Idoppy
NFC
Consequent
1978
$20.⁰⁰

D0851182

COMICS OF THE
AMERICAN WEST

© Editions Dupuis

COMICS OF THE AMERICAN WEST

MAURICE HORN

© Dargaud SA

STOEGER PUBLISHING COMPANY

Copyright © 1977 by Maurice Horn. All rights reserved.

Book design by Richard A. Kenerson

Cover illustration from *Comanche*, by Greg and Hermann, courtesy of the authors.

Library of Congress Cataloging in Publication Data

Horn, Maurice.
    Comics of the American West

    (Stoeger sportsman's library)
    Reprint of the ed. published by Winchester Press, New York
    Bibliography: p.
    Includes index.
    1. Western comic books, strips, etc.—History and criticism.
I. Title.
[PN6714.H67 1978]   741.5′973   77-90767
ISBN 0-88317-048-5

Published by Stoeger Publishing Company
55 Ruta Court
South Hackensack, New Jersey 07606

First Stoeger quality paperback edition, January 1978

This Stoeger Sportsman's Library Edition is published by arrangement with Winchester Press.

Distributed to the book trade by Follett Publishing Company,
1010 West Washington Boulevard, Chicago, Illinois 60607
and to the sporting goods trade by Stoeger Industries,
55 Ruta Court, South Hackensack, New Jersey 07606

In Canada, distributed to the book trade and to the sporting
goods trade by Stoeger Trading Company,
900 Ontario Street East, Montreal, Quebec H2L 1P4

Printed in the United States of America

ACKNOWLEDGMENTS

We wish to extend our thanks to the following persons who have helped in the preparation of this book: Michel Greg, Richard Marschall, S.M. "Jerry" Iger, Leonard Darvin, Bill Blackbeard, Ernesto Traverso, Sheldon Scheps, Denis Gifford and Jørgen Sonnergaard.

Our appreciation also goes to the following organizations for their help and cooperation: King Features Syndicate, the Chicago Tribune, DC Comics Inc, Marvel Comics Group, the Comics Magazine Association of America, Editions Dupuis, Editoriale Corno, Editions du Lombard, and the Academy of Comic Art.

CONTENTS

Coulton Waugh, *Tall Boy*. Courtesy Richard Marschall

INTRODUCTION

© Editions Dupuis

Books devoted to the study and appreciation of comic strips and comic books have appeared in ever-increasing numbers on bookstore shelves in recent years; and so have books dealing with practically every facet and implication of the American West. This phenomenon is not surprising; it was in fact long overdue in view of the deep-seated trend towards the reevaluation of hitherto neglected or scorned forms and aspects of American cultural life and historical experience. Yet, despite the growing acceptance of both the American West and American comic art as basic reflections of the American social and psychological fabric, no book on *Western comics* has ever appeared in print. There have been a number of cogent and well-researched books on the history and aesthetics of Western movies and Western novels, as well as countless essays on the West in history, art and folklore, but on the West in comics, there has been naught. This study, the first ever attempted on this vast and fascinating subject, will endeavor to bridge this regrettable gap.

It has been belatedly acknowledged that the comics—the American comics uppermost—are not an incoherent series of pictures, but the most authentic form of the dreams, hopes, splendors, fears and miseries of our century. It can therefore be induced that the legend and perception of the West (so reflective of the concerns of the age) would constitute a strong undercurrent in the 80-year old history and thematology of the comic form; and this assumption is incontrovertibly borne out in the pages of this book. The comics and the West have always shared, it seems to me, a strong—if subliminal—affinity: just as the Western pioneers were conscious of opening a new geographical frontier, the pioneers of the comics were quick to realize that they were exploring a new artistic frontier. Since many readers of this book may not be well-acquainted with the early history of the comics, and since this history in turn has a strong bearing on the facts, events and incidents chronicled in these pages, it might be well at this juncture to provide some background information on the birth and flowering of this new medium—later called the comics—around the turn of the century.

Ferd Johnson, *Texas Slim* (newspaper strip, USA). © Chicago Tribune-New York News Syndicate.

Europe was first to witness the birth of the illustrated narrative, starting with the 18th-century "cartoons" of William Hogarth, Thomas Rowlandson and James Gillray in England, which were followed in the 19th century by the works of such artists as the Swiss Rodolphe Töpffer, the German Wilhelm Busch, and the French Christophe. But the so-called picture-story was never allowed to fulfill its potential, owing to the European artists' almost slavish devotion to the written word.

Unlike Europe the United States did not cultivate to any such extent the tradition of genteel literariness. American newspapers and magazines displayed a robust, and sometimes rambunctious, vitality to which

Andrija Maurović, *Povratak Starog Mačak* ("The Return of the Old Cat," Yugoslavia). © Andrija Maurović.

editorial cartoonists and pictorial reporters contributed their legitimate share. The Civil War was brought in vivid detail to the American public through the illustrated pages of *Frank Leslie's Illustrated* and *Harper's Bazaar,* just as Frederic Remington and Charles Schreyvogel would later pictorially chronicle the opening of the Western frontier.

Particularly significant was the popularity of the humor magazines, *Puck, Judge,* and *Life,* in whose pages could already be found the artists later made famous through the comics: Rudolph Dirks, Richard Outcault, F.B. Opper. At the same time the American daily newspapers, competing for readership, brought forth the Sunday supplements, which made increasing use of illustration and color. Now, almost at the end of the 19th century, all conditions looked right for the bursting forth of a new form of communication, which would be neither quite literature nor purely graphic art, but would freely borrow from both.

To answer the growing demand for illustrators and cartoonists, new and sometimes untried talent was brought to the fore, producing the necessary artistic ferment required for all radical departures from the

Walter Molino, *Kit Carson* (Italy). ©
Mondadori.

accepted norm. The importing of new and more advanced presses from Europe allowed the newspapers to print more copies, better and faster, and to reach an ever-increasing public. The enormous influx of immigrants from eastern and southern Europe, with little or no knowledge of the English language, gave the medium of visual communication a steady and safe public, free from the shibboleths of literary forms. Finally, the circulation wars among newspapers also worked to the advantage of the artist who, unlike his writing colleague, had a style that could be recognized at first glance.

The often-recounted struggle between the two giants of American journalism, Joseph Pulitzer and William Randolph Hearst, with the protagonists luring employees away from each other, and putting more and more reliance on their Sunday supplements, provided the final catalyst in the synthesis of the disparate elements of narrative and illustration. In a matter of months a new art form was born.

Even the exact date of this birth, however, has been clouded in controversy. Both Richard Outcault and James Swinnerton can lay claim to the distinction of having "invented" the comics. As early as 1892 Swinnerton had created *Little Bears and Tykes*, a series depicting in continuing sequence the adventures of a merry crew of assorted urchin and animal characters, thus renewing and updating the great cartoon tradition of the English masters. Outcault used text and dialogue within the picture, and his *Yellow Kid* (from which the term "yellow journalism" is derived) definitively established the viability of the form around 1896.

The greatest contributor to the new medium, however, was Rudolph Dirks, whose *Katzenjammer Kids* (loosely based on Busch's *Max und Moritz*) was the first comic strip to make full and systematic use of the balloon as main support of the accompanying dialogue. Indeed, thanks to Dirks's efforts, the balloon has become the instantly recognizable trademark of the comic strip.

It fell to F.B. Opper (who, unlike the 20-year-old Dirks, was already a cartoonist of some distinction) to sum up the possibilities of the form in a number of comic creations, among which *Happy Hooligan* (1900) is the best remembered.

Thus the four artists mentioned above can be rightly called "the fathers of the comics." Around 1900, thanks to the pioneering spirit of these men, the comics were already in possession of a basic vocabulary and a recognizable set of conventions, and were evolving their own vital syntax. The whole process had taken place in a matter of a few years, truly a remarkable achievement.

Hermann and Greg, *Comanche* (Belgium).
© Editions du Lombard.

In the course of the 20th century, as we all know, the comics have been sprouting in all directions, encompassing not only slapstick and humor, but adventure (including, of course, Western adventure), human interest, social relevance, philosophical musing, and speculative fiction as well. The comics have gone on to become a mainstay of American newspapers, and, from the late Thirties on, have constituted a phenomenally successful facet of popular literature in the form of comic books. Nor have the comics remained the exclusive province of the United States: they have spread to the remotest corners of the globe, and every major (and not so major) country in the world can now boast of a national comics production (sometimes excellent, and often flourishing.) Along with movies and television, the comics are a universal medium.

It is not coincidental that the rise in the worldwide popularity of the comics should have been paralleled by the increase in the fascination that the American West has come to hold on a great number of the population of this planet. Starting with Buffalo Bill's Wild West shows, the history and legend that form the West have inexorably entered our global consciousness. In literature the crude, but diverting, dime novels of E.Z.C. Judson have been followed by the much more sophisticated sagebrush sagas of Zane Grey and Luke Short, right down to the contemporary fiction of Louis L'Amour, whose readership far surpasses that of any living author; while David Belasco's stageplay, *The Girl of the Golden West*, received such worldwide acclaim in the early years of this century that Puccini made it into an opera.

Gir (Jean Giraud) and Jean Michel Charlier,
Lieutenant Blueberry (France). © Editions Dargaud.

The movies have long since adopted the Western story as their own to such an extent that the development of the Western film is practically inseparable from that of the world cinema—particularly the American cinema. D.W. Griffith, Thomas Ince and John Ford are only a few among the many directors who learned and perfected their skills on the Western; and Westerns have formed the backbone of Hollywood grade-B movies and serials, just as they have later played an important role in the development of television dramatic series.

In art the West has proved a primordial source of inspiration to countless American painters and sculptors whose works, after a long period of unjust neglect, are now being eagerly sought after by museums and private collectors. No facet of contemporary life has remained immune to the lure of the West, as the growing popularity of Western-and-country music, and the spread of Western lifestyles throughout the world, amply demonstrate. In the fourth edition of *The History of Winchester Firearms* the authors wrote, for instance, that, "Western Europe . . . was undergoing a sort of Wild West boom. There were western dude ranches, indian and cowboy replicas, special stores catering to western-style clothing, 'frontier towns' and special vacations based on an 'Old West' theme." (The author could also have added Japan, Yugoslavia and the Latin American countries to the list of countries enjoying this Western revival.)

All these developments point even more acutely toward the need for a serious and comprehensive study of the West in the comics. In our attempt at answering this need we have devoted separate chapters to the history of Western newspaper strips, Western comic books, and foreign Westerns; while a separate chapter also documents the pervasive presence of the West in the whole body of American comic art. Finally we have capped this study with a summary of Western themes and inspirations as they run through the comics of the American West, and, conversely, we have tried to show the important contribution made by the comics to the mythology of the American West.

Beyond its formal purpose, however, we have tried to make this an entertaining book. The recall of nostalgic names out of the comics' past—The Lone Ranger, Red Ryder, King of the Mounties—should bring back happy memories to many of the readers; while the more than 200 illustrations that grace the book probably form the greatest iconographic field ever assembled on the subject—a whirlpool of unforgettable images.

Hugo Pratt, *Sgt. Kirk* (Argentina). © Editorial Abril.

CHAPTER ONE

A SHORT HISTORY OF THE WESTERN STRIP

© K.F.S.

Setting the scene

The iconography of the American West goes almost as far back as the exploration of the vast subcontinent itself. The Stephen H. Long expedition of 1819 included two painters among its team: the already established Samuel Seymour of Philadelphia and the twenty-year old Titian Ramsey Peale, the first artist to depict the Rocky Mountains in painting. They were followed by many others over the years: the Swiss-born Peter Rindisbacher, John Mix Stanley, Alfred Jacob Miller, Friedrich Kurz are only a few of the names that come readily to mind. Most notable of all was George Catlin, famous for his gallery of portraits depicting Indian chieftains in full regalia.

These and many other artists blazed a trail and fired up the imaginations of several generations of American boys. Among them were Frederic Remington (1861–1909) and Charles Russell (1864–1926) whose pictorial descriptions of the West, its traditions and its legends, formed the bedrock upon which every later Western artist was, by necessity, to build. So overwhelming have Remington's and Russell's legacies proved to be that they have obscured for a long time the names of other artists of the Western scene; their influence has extended far beyond the graphic and pictural traditions, and can be detected in almost any Western movie, and particularly in those films directed by John Ford.

Of more direct bearing on the then-nascent comic strip form, however, were the humble but colorful covers of Western dime novels. Colonel William "Buffalo Bill" Cody was a favorite subject for these covers and he was often depicted sitting regally on his white horse. The artists who did the covers and the interior art for these cheap editions were often surprisingly good. None was better or more gifted, however, than the German Charles Henckel who, in the 1890's, did a series of remarkable drawings ("from life," the publisher claimed) for the fictional *Buffalo Bill and His Wild West*. Henckel's depictions of cowboys riding the range, breaking bucking bronchos, and battling Indians (drawings which were often enclosed in square or rectangular frames) foreshadowed the works of later comic strip artists.

Charles Henckel, *Buffalo Bill and His Wild West*. Henckel's drawings of cowboys riding, breaking bucking broncos and battling Indians often foreshadowed the works of later comic strip artists. Courtesy the Academy of Comic Art.

The beginning of the Western tradition in comics

The West—as a state of mind—was not, of course, unknown to the early cartoonists. The opening of the

western frontier was still fresh in the memories of Americans of the turn of the century, and the movies had already latched onto the theme (*The Great Train Robbery* dates back to 1903). C.W. Kahles, the first comic artist to use suspense as a story-telling device, made the West and its conventions (already well-established in dime novels and stage plays of the late 19th and early 20th century) the background of the very first adventure of his *Hairbreadth Harry* (1906); so a little later did Harry Hershfield in *Desperate Desmond* (1910). The West was also explored (or touched upon) in such diverse strips as Lyonel Feininger's *The Kinder-Kids*, George McManus's *Panhandle Pete*, and Rudolph Dirks's *The Katzenjammer Kids* (there was an hilarious sequence, running for almost a full year in 1909-10, in which the Kids came up against a band of conniving Indians, unflappable cowhands, and daffy Mexican desperadoes).

The cartoonist who made most constant reference to the West in the early years of the newspaper strip was James Swinnerton, himself a native of California. As early as 1897, for instance, he had his famous "Journal Tigers" (all of them in cowboy attire and ten-gallon hats) holding up a mail coach and indulging in other shenanigans associated with "the wild Wild West." In 1902 Swinnerton, on advice from his doctor, settled in Arizona, and Western scenes started to show up with greater and greater regularity in his work, especially in *Little Jimmy.*

James Swinnerton, *Little Jimmy*. *Little Jimmy* started as a boy strip in 1904, but soon evolved into the first genuine Western strip. Its locale was the Great Desert of the Southwest. © King Features Syndicate.

Using the ploy of having little Jimmy Thompson and his family go to the desert for vacation, Swinnerton indulged his love for the landscape, flora and fauna of Arizona and Nevada. Later *Little Jimmy* would permanently shift its locale to the Southwest, making it the first genuine Western strip. There Jimmy was to meet some of his more constant companions including a little Navaho Indian, an older Indian brave named Somolo, and Li'l Ole Bear, Jimmy's pet bear cub. At the same time, Swinnerton gave even wider rein to his fascination for desert and Indian life and lore in *Canyon Kiddies*, a series of weekly panels he did for *Good Housekeeping* in the Teens and Twenties. These were full of mystery, happenings and wonders, and helped establish further the Western scene as a familiar element of the comic strip medium.

Following in the wake of Swinnerton's creations, the Twenties witnessed a modest boom in things Western among comic strip artists. From that time on, no comic strip continuity was complete without one or more stories set in the West (some of these will be described in greater detail in a further chapter). It was then also that the Western began to emerge as a distinct comic strip genre, with its conventions, rituals, and formulas. Why the comics should have been so late in establishing a Western tradition, when the movies had been at it for almost two decades is a matter of some speculation; it would seem that the film treatment of the West had been so overwhelming as to leave scant room for any other medium of visual narration—Western painting, for instance, suffered a long eclipse during the same years.

J.R. Williams, the creator of *Out Our Way*, had known an adventurous career prior to his becoming a cartoonist. In the course of his tribulations he once worked as a cowhand on the Frank McMurray Ranch of White Sands, New Mexico. He later went to Oklahoma and then joined the United States cavalry, all the while storing away experiences and memories that were to serve him well during his tenure on *Out Our Way*.

Out Our Way (created in 1921 for NEA Service) was not a comic strip in the strict sense, but consisted of daily panels with a strong sense of continuity from day to day and week to week. Within the framework of his panel, Williams developed a number of sub-series ("Born Thirty Years Too Soon," "Why Mothers Get

J.R. Williams, *Out Our Way*. A number of Williams's famous panels were devoted to a memorable group of cowboy characters and to the humorous, but affectionate, depiction of cowboy life. © NEA Service.

Gray," and "The Worry Wart" are among the best-remembered), including one—possibly the most famous one—with no separate running title, about a group of memorable cowboy characters. This series ran for over 30 years and, in the words of Western historian Ed Ainsworth, "it embodied the essence of all [Williams] had observed and learned on cattle ranches, the full flavor of his own personality and sense of humor."

The Western action of *Out Our Way* was most often humorous, carried on as it was by such outrageous (and wonderfully named) characters as Smoky, Curly, Stiffy, Cotton, Spuds, Soda, not to mention the redoubtable mount Jiggin' Jack, and the ubiquitous Schoolmarm. Yet, when there was action, it was depicted with matter-of-fact realism, even brutality. In 1924 Williams showed a scene full of dead bodies (the first instance of corpses being depicted in a comic strip, according to Bill Blackbeard). In another episode, the hunting down of coyotes was documented with a wealth of graphic details definitely not for the squeamish. In this respect *Out Our Way* can be considered the direct forerunner of the action-filled Westerns of the Thirties. (A good selection of J.R. Williams's Western vignettes was published by Scribner's under the title *Cowboys Out Our Way*.)

Ferd Johnson, *Texas Slim*. Johnson's 1925 creation was possibly the first Western parodic strip, a genre now in full bloom. © Chicago Tribune-New York News Syndicate.

The Twenties also saw the birth of the parodic Western, a genre now in full bloom. The first such (or at least consistently such) was undoubtedly Ferd Johnson's *Texas Slim*, started in the Chicago *Tribune* in 1925. Texas Slim was an exuberant, outgoing ranch hand with a knack for landing in trouble. Along with his cowboy buddy, a rather untidy, bemoustached saddle tramp known (with good reason) as Dirty Dalton, he managed to wreak havoc on his boss, Mr. Akers's cattle spread in Texas. Then the scene shifted to an unnamed city (clearly Chicago), a good occasion for Johnson to indulge in some low humor, with Texas and Dirty playing their tricks on the unsuspecting denizens of the Windy City. Particularly funny were Slim's ham-handed attempts at courting Mr. Akers's daughter, Jessie. Despite its title, the strip's star attraction turned out to be the uncouth Dalton with his unreconstructed but ingratiating ways of dealing with every emergency with a closed mind and an open mouth.

Texas Slim was dropped in 1928, briefly re-surfaced as a gag strip in 1932, and was revived again in 1940 (an account of the strip's further tribulations is given later on. See "The Fearless Forties.")

An unlikely contributor to the Western comic strip was Johnny Gruelle (the creator of *Raggedy Ann and Andy*) who originated *Brutus* in 1928. *Brutus* can probably claim the distinction of being the weirdest Western strip ever concocted. Gruelle drew it in a whimsical, oddly un-geometrical style. His characters had tilted facial features and sported ill-fitting or wholly unaccountable pieces of clothing. Derby-hatted and cigar-chomping animals were running all across the page, involved in obscure pursuits whose relevance to the main narrative were never made clear. The plots were just as unpredictable as the drawings. The action ostensibly took place on a cattle spread called the Hot Dog Ranch. Brutus was a diminutive character of amazing strength, and his feats foreshadowed those of the later Popeye the Sailor. He had as companions the slow-witted Sampson and Lilly Hoss, a weirdly-shaped, funny-acting creature presented by Gruelle as a mare. The action was full of non-sequiturs and outlandish situations (at one point Lilly Hoss gulped down a bottle of hair lotion and ran around looking like a sheepdog). *Brutus*, unfortunately, never even approached the fantasy of *Krazy Kat* or the wit of *Thimble Theater*, and has been largely ignored by historians (it disappeared in 1938).

Once the pattern of story continuity had been established in the Western strip, new creations were bound to follow. One such was *Mescal Ike*, the collaboration of scriptwriter S.L. Huntley and cartoonist Art Huhta in 1928. The early continuity was straight adventure with large doses of rambunctious humor. Attired in a white ten-gallon hat and Mexican chaps, Mescal could be counted on to keep peace and order around the ramshackle desert town grandly known as Cactus Center. In his endeavors (which included, at one time or other, restoring a gold mine deed to its rightful owner, putting a band of thieving night-riders out of business,

Johnny Gruelle, *Brutus*. The weirdest Western strip ever concocted, *Brutus* was the brainchild of Johnny Gruelle, creator of *Raggedy Ann and Andy*. © Herald-Tribune Syndicate.

and rescuing the newly-arriving schoolmarm from runaway horses) Mescal was assisted by his bedraggled buddy, Dirty Shirt Mulloney, who cracked most of the jokes and stole most of the scenes.

S.L. Huntley and Art Huhta, *Mescal Ike*. This strip was based on a series of humorous columns that Huntley had been writing under the *nom-de-plume* "Mescal Ike."
© S.L. Huntley.

Mescal Ike was not too successful as a continuity strip and, following a change of syndicates, the authors turned to a conventional gag format. The two protagonists then got upstaged by the larcenous shenanigans of Pa Piffle, the bewhiskered owner of the Busy Bee Cafe, and a scoundrel at heart. *Mescal Ike*'s authors never quite made up their minds whether to keep the story on a straight course or play it for laughs. Accordingly *Mescal Ike* was never grippingly suspenseful nor rollickingly funny. Some of its early adventures were entertaining and fast-paced, however, and they prefigured the action-filled plots of the Thirties. The new format did not work too well either, and after a brief try at continuity again, Huntley and Huhta called it quits in 1940.

The explosion of the Thirties

The Thirties have been called—with good reason—"the adventurous decade." Adventure strips flourished in this period as in no time before or since. This was the epoch of *Flash Gordon*, *Terry and the Pirates*, *Prince Valiant*, and countless others. The Western strip also enjoyed a boom during the decade. Unfortunately, the first cowboy feature to come out of the Thirties (in 1930 precisely) did not turn out to be a trailblazer, or even a very good example of the genre: it was Harry O'Neill's *Broncho Bill* (to give it the title by which it is best known.)

Harry O'Neill, *Broncho Bill*. The strip concerned itself with the doings of a daring band of teenage vigilantes known as the "Rangers," and led by the title character.
© United Feature Syndicate.

The strip started as *Young Buffalo Bill,* then was briefly changed to *Buckaroo Bill,* before acquiring its definitive title by the middle of the decade (perhaps as a left-handed tribute to the first Western movie star, Broncho Bill Anderson).

The action of the strip took place in a geographical area at the foot of the Rockies, possibly in Montana (some episodes have the mountains as background, others the plains), at the time of the Civil War. In order to help the local sheriff cope with the influx of outlaws caused by the war, and in the absence of most men of military age, Bill had organized a corps of youthful vigilantes known as "the Rangers." Bill and his teen-age cohorts saw no paucity of action what with claim-jumpers, cattle rustlers, bank robbers and other miscreants abounding all over the place. One of the more entertaining adventures dealt with a gang of counterfeiters intent on framing the sheriff for the false silver coinage they themselves were circulating. Young Bill, however, saw through the scheme and cleared the sheriff in the nick of time, just as the lawman was about to be lynched by an infuriated mob.

Despite his young age, Bill could outdraw any man west of the Missouri (he once shot the glasses out of the hands of a half-dozen outlaws with a single bullet) and, mounted on his faithful stallion Blackie, was able to outrun any pursuing foe. Bill's enemies often made the mistake of kidnapping him, but the young ranger would somehow always manage to get loose, and return with reinforcements to fall upon the unwitting bandits.

Harry O'Neill's draftsmanship was not on a par with his ambitions, and neither was his writing. His graphic style was limp and his action scenes lacked punch at the climax; the narrative and dialogue were written in an atrocious style. Yet there were some nice documentary touches in *Broncho Bill:* for instance, the protagonists were (correctly) armed with the 1851 model Colt instead of the more classic (but anachronistic) 1873 model depicted in most Western strips and movies. Also the U.S. cavalry was seen as playing a great role in restoring order to the West, as was historically the case during and immediately after the Civil War days.

In spite of its numerous handicaps, *Broncho Bill* managed to last for about two decades, only disappearing in the late Forties.

Of a far different caliber was *Little Joe,* created by Ed Leffingwell on October 1, 1933, for the Chicago Tribune-New York News Syndicate. Like *Broncho Bill,* *Little Joe* had a teen-aged boy as its main protagonist; but the resemblance stopped there. The strip was set

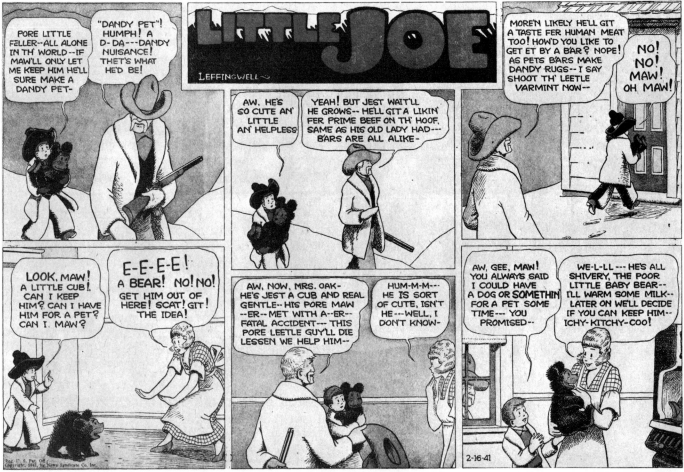

Ed Leffingwell, *Little Joe.* © Chicago Tribune-New York News Syndicate.

in the cattle country of the contemporary West and, stylistically as well as narratively, was light-years removed from the simpleness of *Broncho Bill.* Ed Leffingwell was Harold Gray's cousin (and assistant), and the resemblance between *Little Joe* and *Little Orphan Annie* was not coincidental. As Bill Blackbeard (writing of the strip in *The World Encyclopedia of Comics*) clearly demonstrated, Gray had a strong hand in the plotting and dialoguing of the strip, and even drew some of the main characters' faces. "Effectively, *Little Joe* must be regarded as an additional Gray strip," Blackbeard states, "from its inception in 1933 to at least 1946."

Little Joe Oak lived on his widowed mother's ranch which was managed by a gruff character (and former gunfighter) named Utah. Soon Joe and Utah found themselves involved in innumerable adventures, some of them humorous and others melodramatic, like the one in which Utah and Joe outsmarted a pair of shyster lawyers from the East who were trying to defraud Mrs. Oak of her title to the ranch with the help of forged documents.

Harold Gray never lost an opportunity of poking political fun at the various dude types who came to visit Joe's ranch. Trade unions were Gray's special béte noire, and he never tired of taking potshots at them, variously comparing them to rattlesnakes or buzzards intent on seeing the cattle dispatched in order to pick the carrion. In the late Thirties he added to the strip's *dramatis personae* the comic figure of a Mexican general (simply known as Ze Gen'ral), the better to pick on politicians of the New Deal by using the situation in Mexico as a thinly disguised parable of political developments in Washington, as Gray saw them.

During WWII Joe, Utah and Ze Gen'ral joined with gusto the fight against the Axis powers. Characteristically theirs was a private war, in which our heroes rounded up assorted gangs of alien spies or home-grown fifth-columnists, and even captured a landing party of Japanese saboteurs whom Utah, with his usual business acumen, put to work on his ranch (at no pay, of course).

After 1946, *Little Joe*, now entirely done by Ed Leffingwell, and after his death by his brother Robert, reverted to a weekly gag format. It lost most of its appeal, and finally disappeared towards the end of the Fifties.

Little Joe should be remembered chiefly for its always intelligent, often arresting, narratives of the

Garrett Price, *White Boy*. This strip is notable for its qualities of design and composition. © Chicago Tribune-New York News Syndicate.

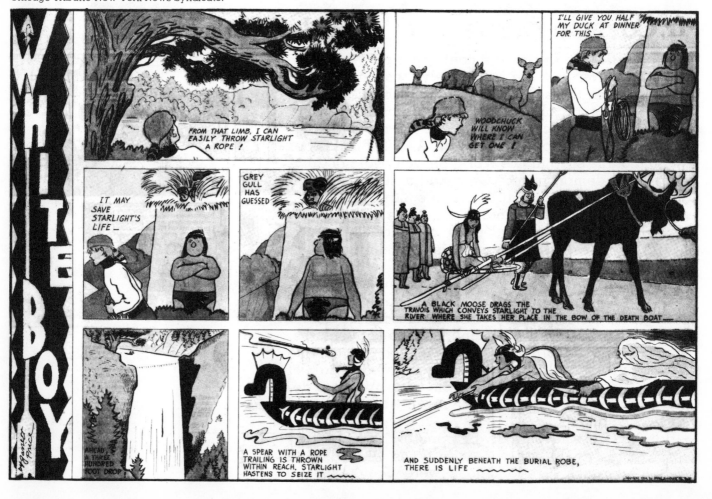

Thirties and early Forties, as well as for Leffingwell's subtle, but masterly, depiction of western scenes, from rides through craggy and awe-inspiring canyons to wild stampedes across the limitless expanses of prairie country. It is certainly a minor classic and can even be regarded as the forerunner of many Western strips of the Sixties and Seventies.

Only a short week after the inception of *Little Joe*, the News-Tribune Syndicate came up with another off-beat Western series, Garrett Price's *White Boy*, a Sunday half-page as stunning as it is obscure. Garrett Price, who was then working in the *Tribune* art department, was asked to do a Western strip by the syndicate. The syndicate's stricture that the feature should appeal primarily to a juvenile audience proved an albatross around Price's neck from the start. "I was hampered by authentic knowledge of the West," Price later confided. "My folks . . . left Kansas when I was a year old. Until I was nineteen we lived in Wyoming, Oklahoma, South Dakota—mostly in Wyoming." The artist, however, set to work with a sense of purpose and an undeniable vision of what the strip should be.

Set in the late 19th century the strip had its adolescent hero (simply known as White Boy) captured by the Sioux, then rescued by a rival tribe, nursed to health and loved by an Indian girl named Chickadee. Even after a scout, Dan Brown, enters the story, White Boy decides to stay with his Indian friends.

The storyline was an amalgam of Indian lore and legend (how the snowshoe rabbit got his fur, for instance), gag situations often involving White Boy's pet bear Whimper, and some genuinely gripping narratives, such as the famous tale of the white "Moon Queen" lording it over an utterly cowed tribe of red men. The main appeal of the strip, however, was Price's incredibly evocative artwork. The artist would often draw in a flat, patterned line, dominated by earth colors, in a style reminiscent of Indian sand paintings. His horses, cattle and buffaloes were frozen in the hieratic pose of animals in cave drawings. His light was sometimes subdued, sometimes dazzling, in harmony with the days and the seasons.

Then in 1935, on instructions from the syndicate, Price switched his strip to the modern locale of a dude ranch. Chickadee and the other Indian characters were dropped, White Boy became Bob White, and a new heroine by the name of Doris Hale was introduced. The strip, rechristened *Whiteboy in Skull Valley*, and later simply *Skull Valley* (there is an actual place called Skull Valley in Arizona) turned into a routine Western with the usual stories about cattle rustlers, bank robbers and masked bandits. Price did his best to sustain the interest of his readers, but when *Skull Valley* degenerated into a tired gag feature, he decided to quit, later concentrating on a successful career as a *New Yorker* cartoonist and magazine illustrator. The last *Skull Valley* page appeared on August 16, 1936.

Western strips continued to be produced at a fast clip all throughout the Thirties. There was *Way Out West* by Clyde (better known as "Vic") Forsythe whom King Features had induced away from *Joe Jinks*. Born in California, Forsythe also had a good knowledge of the West, and in this semi-humorous series he succeeded in introducing authentic elements of the Southwestern scene. His burros, especially, were drawn with a fine eye for comedy. Unfortunately, Forsythe had a peculiar drawing style better suited for slapstick than for action. Somehow he always managed to foreshorten his figures with the result that his cowboys looked like midgets mounted on Shetland ponies. *Way Out West*, started in 1933, lasted for only a few short years.

Vic Forsythe, *Way Out West*. © King Features Syndicate.

Another early casualty was the far more interesting *Ted Strong* which saw the light of print in 1935. Drawn by Al Carreño in a loose, forceful style, Ted Strong was a taciturn, fast-acting hero, not unlike some of the screen characters played by Gary Cooper. His adventures (which took place in modern times) involved fast-riding horse chases, hair-raising escapes and some of the most entertaining gun battles ever depicted on a newspaper page. The strip unfortunately did not last long; the last newspaper page appeared in 1938 (the hero had by then become an undercover agent). Ted

Al Carreño, *Ted Strong*. Almost completely ignored in its country of origin, *Ted Strong* was much better appreciated in Europe (here it can be seen in its French Version). © George Matthew Adams Service.

Strong however, still drawn by Carreño, was to continue his career in comic books for a while.

The parodic Western also continued to flourish. Allen Saunders (scriptwriter) and Elmer Woggon (artist) produced *Big Chief Wahoo* in late 1936. At first the title character was a cigar-stand Indian used as a stooge by a medicine show operator named the Great Gusto. Eventually the Great Gusto faded out of the strip and Wahoo, along with his sweetheart Minnie-Ha-Cha, a former nightclub singer, pursued his humorous exploits within the setting of an Indian reservation. In the Forties Wahoo was gradually edged out in his turn by a blond private eye named Steve Roper. The strip, now called *Steve Roper and Nomad*, is no longer set in the West.

Another attempt at Western humor was *Pecos Bill, Mighty Man of the West!* distributed by the George Matthew Adams Service. The strip was drawn in a disjointed style by Jack Warren (who signed "JAW")

Elmer Woggon and Allen Saunders, *Big Chief Wahoo.* © Field Newspaper Syndicate.

Jack Warren and Tex O'Reilly, *Pecos Bill, Mighty Man of the West!* This strip was a poor attempt at spoofing one of the West's most legendary figures, and it misfired. © George Matthew Adams Service.

Zane Grey and Jack Abbott, *Desert Gold.* This was one among the many comic strip serializations of Zane Grey's novels. © Register and Tribune Syndicate.

and written by Tex O'Reilly in a prose that can only be (charitably) called strained. "Gangway you ghouls!" Pecos Bill would exclaim to startled buzzards. "Wag them wings." This poor attempt at spoofing one of the West's most legendary figures was of mercifully short duration.

Zane Grey in the comics

In the Thirties Zane Grey was the foremost Western novelist, with scores of books and film scripts to his credit. The comics did not fail to take notice of Grey's appeal to the readers and, starting in 1933, serialization of his stories (*Nevada, Desert Gold*, etc.) appeared in newspaper strip form, syndicated by the Register and Tribune Syndicate and drawn by the undistinguished Jack Abbott. The series was still running by the end of 1934 when Stephen Slesinger, a promoter, merchandiser and talent agent, approached Grey with an offer to create an original Western strip for King Features Syndicate. Loosely based on one of Grey's magazine stories, *King of the Royal Mounted* subsequently saw the light of print (as a Sunday page) in February 1935.

Sergeant King (that was his name, not a nickname) must have been the most dedicated Mountie on the force; no sooner had he completed one dangerous mission that his superior, gruff but understanding Inspector McKenzie (McKenzie-King, a bit of political levity on the part of Grey here) sent him back on another. King worked out of the Mounted Police headquarters in Vancouver, B.C., but his beat encompassed all of western Canada, the Yukon and the Northwest Territories. In the first episode (probably the only one written by Grey himself) King rescued Betty Blake and her brother Kid from the clutches of Ike Sling's gang of outlaws who were trying to cheat them out of their inheritance. At the end of the adventure King and Betty ended up in what was regarded as the Sunday comic equivalent of a clinch; this ending might have been appropriate to a magazine story, but proved to be a nuisance in a long-running comic strip whose hero was best left unattached. Betty would make periodic re-appearances in King's life, but her status remained purposely vague, and she was finally written out of the script. Kid, on the other hand, was to become King's inseparable boy companion.

King of the Royal Mounted's cast of characters was rounded out with Pilot Jerry Laroux. A French-Canadian, Laroux inevitably sported a moustache. In the early episodes he spoke normal English but was later made to use a regrettable pidgin ("Oui. Mebbe he know too much about what happen to Corporal

Dale.") Otherwise he was a consumate flyer, a loyal comrade-in-arms and a good man to have around in a pinch. In a few instances he even upstaged King (as occasionally Kid also did).

Zane Grey and Allen Dean, *King of the Royal Mounted*. © King Features Syndicate.

King himself, however, remained the star of the strip. While determined, righteous and fearless, in the mold of the classic hero, King was in many ways an unlikely hero as well. There was a wistfulness, a vulnerability in his countenance; and his sad, long face reflected a world-weariness at variance with the breezy self-assurance of most comic strip heroes. He was taciturn, and never cracked a joke or a smile, yet there was something oddly appealing about him, the slightest hint that there lived a man—perhaps a wounded man—under the uniform.

King would sometimes get involved in stories of straight detection, such as uncovering a jewel thief among the guests at a posh resort hotel ("The Mystery of the Kobee Diamond," 1937), or in tales of espionage, thwarting, for instance, the sinister designs of foreign agents plying the waters of British Columbia in a U-Boat ("The Steel Shark," 1939); but most of the action remained true to the themes and conventions of the Western genre. There were plenty of ferocious gunfights, breath-taking horse-rides, ambushes and chases. The plots were often involved (reflecting Zane Grey's) but always absorbing. There was no padding there as the action proceeded at a furious pace from one incident to the next. As the Belgian scriptwriter Greg once admiringly observed: "Some episodes of a few pages [in *King*] contain enough material for a 40 or 60 page series in today's comic strips."

King's foes ran the gamut from fur-thieves, cattle rustlers and crooked Indian traders to mad scientists, industrial saboteurs and ruthless land grabbers. The action was violent, and death a common-place occurrence. For instance, in one 1936 daily strip an entire family was murdered in cold blood by a roving gang of outlaws. Yet the villains were not always shown as irremediably lost. There was a strong sense of redemption running through the series, as former criminal characters would pay for their life of crime by making the supreme sacrifice. Thus the renegade Ned Thorpe would give up his life while detaining the outlaws launched in hot pursuit of his sister Judy and her protector King; and Thaddeus Harper, "the Emperor," would get gunned down standing up to the very gang of cut-throats he himself had raised.

King of the Royal Mounted was set in modern times, but the appurtenances of the modern world (cars, submarines, movies, etc.) did not intrude appreciably into what was essentially a universe of the outdoors, at least not until the late Forties. Even Laroux's plane was seen mainly as a convenient means of getting to one's assignment fast. Most of the time King would travel on horseback or by husky-drawn sled. The scenery was one of the great assets of the strip with its lovingly detailed snow-capped peaks, vast plain expanses and limitless snowfields. There was genuine excitement also in the use of real place-names. Great Bear Lake, Peace River, Cariboo Mountains, Dawson, Yellowknife—those sang in memory as no made-up name could. And then there were all the familiar *clichés* of the far North: grey wolves and plumed Indians, grizzly bears and fur-parkaed Eskimos, to add to the exoticism.

The first artist on the strip was Allen Dean who drew the Sunday page from its inception till 1936, and the daily strip from its start in 1936 till 1938. He was succeeded by Charles Flanders who turned the strip over to Jim Gary in 1939. Both Flanders and Gary were solid craftsmen; Flanders's tenure was characterized by a stiffening of the characters while Gary was looser, more relaxed. However he too incurred the curse of the comic strip artist: hiring ghosts to draw for

Zane Grey and Charles Flanders, *King of the Royal Mounted.* © King Features Syndicate.

him. First was John Wade Hampton, then Rodlow Willard, one of the most hapless of strip cartoonists, who made a shambles of the series until its ultimate demise in 1955.

King of the Royal Mounted is chiefly remembered for Allen Dean's solid, and at times brilliant, artwork. Dean was an incomparable depicter of animals. His horses were especially striking, but he was equally adept at evoking the menace of a pack of wolves howling in the polar night, or the serenity of a family of deer drinking at a mountain stream. His line was sometimes clumsy, but his sense of composition was graceful and airy. He could, like no other, render the bluish immensity of the northern snowfields against which King's uniform burned bright.

Zane Grey (or someone) must have felt the same way about Dean's artistic abilities—when Grey unveiled his newest comic strip confection in 1936, a Sunday half-page called *Tex Thorne*, Allen Dean was chosen to illustrate it.

Zane Grey and Jim Gary, *King of the Royal Mounted*. Gary was the last and the longest-lasting of the illustrators who drew the adventures of the famous Mountie created by Zane Grey. © King Features Syndicate.

Tex Thorne was a much more conventional Western than *King*, and contained the usual Grey plot ingredients. Tex was a gunfighter who hired out his gun for justice, not money. His first task was to clean out West Texas from the menace of the dreaded outlaw Jed Blackstone. Spurning the love of his boss's daughter, Anita Wayne, he then followed the mysterious girl who had saved his life on two previous occasions on her errand of vengeance against his old enemy (and the girl's former lover) Colt Ashton. Again victorious, Tex would once more leave the town he had just pacified, impervious to the entreaties of his friends, and the imploring glances of the girl, Susan Locke, to go on his appointed rounds . . .

Tex Thorne was not the usual Erroll Flynn-type of hero. He had qualms of conscience, and he actually foreshadowed a familiar figure of latter-day movie Westerns such as *Shane*, that of the morally troubled gunfighter. After the gunning down of one of his foes he once confided to his only trusted friend (characteristically it was his horse): "Another notch in my gun handle to haunt me nights, Topaz." He would sometimes hunger for a more sedate life, and he was al-

Zane Grey and Allen Dean, Tex Thorne. Tex Thorne *was a rugged, rough and sometimes brutal Western that unfortunately did not last.* © King Features Syndicate.

most tempted when Anita pleaded with him. Yet, in the end, he could only answer a higher calling. "Sorry, ma'am," he would simply reply, "but the grass won't just grow under my feet."

Allen Dean depicted the adventures of this latter-day knight errant with his usual economy of line and his flair for authentic detail. The feature, however, did not click with the readers; perhaps the action was too straightforward, too sparse. At any rate *Tex Thorne* lasted for less than a year, disappearing early in 1937. Allen Dean went on working on the *King* daily strip for one more year, then disappeared from sight. Despite multiple enquiries and painstaking research, no information has yet turned up on this talented and enigmatic artist.

The Lone Ranger rides again! (and again)

In the Thirties King Features was the MGM of newspaper syndicates. The policy there was to have at least two entries in every major strip category. In 1938 the syndicate editors bought the adaptation rights to Fran Striker's fabulously successful creation, *The Lone Ranger*. The new feature made its debut (both daily and Sunday) in September 1938.

Ever since the Lone Ranger had first ridden the airwaves its success had been phenomenal. It had begun on January 30, 1933, on Detroit's radio station WXYZ, carried on the strains of the *William Tell* overture.

Also in 1938 William Witney and John English had produced the first (and the best) screen version of the radio series, so King wasn't taking any undue chances. In fact, the Lone Ranger's origin was so well known to readers through radio and film that the strip's scriptwriters did not even bother to tell it again. The tale is worth retelling here, however.

One dark day in the 1880's, a group of six Texas Rangers led by Captain Dan Reid was ambushed by

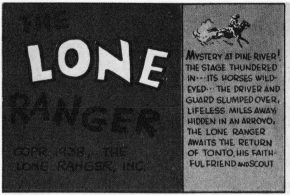

Ed Kressy, *The Lone Ranger*. Ed Kressy was the first artist on the *Lone Ranger* newspaper strip. Kressy's drawings had an awkward quality that fitted in well with the loose script. © King Features Syndicate.

the murderous gang of Butch Cavendish. All the Rangers were killed with the exception of the captain's younger brother John who was rescued by the Indian Tonto. To deceive Cavendish Tonto dug six graves, one for each of the Rangers. John Reid, once he had been nursed back to health, donned a mask so he would not be recognized, and solemnly vowed vengeance on the Cavendish gang and on all evil-doers. Thus was the legend of the Lone Ranger born.

The first artist on the *Lone Ranger* strip was the much-maligned Ed Kressy. While Kressy can hardly be regarded as a great (or even good) cartoonist, his drawings had an awkward quality, a spontaneity that well fitted the loose script (at first written by Striker himself). In the early weeks of 1939 Kressy was replaced, however, by Charles Flanders, who had cut his teeth on *King of the Royal Mounted*. Flanders did a creditable job on the strip, and his characterization of the masked avenger must be accounted the definitive one. His long tenure on the strip (over 30 years!) unfortunately caused him to grow disenchanted and careless, and from the late Fifties on, *The Lone Ranger* often lapsed into unintended self-parody (when it was not ghosted outright by other hands).

The title "Lone Ranger" was always something of a misnomer since the hero had in actuality at least two constant companions. The first one was the faithful Tonto (to whom the Lone Ranger was "Kemo Sabay," the Trusty Scout) who often would accept torture rather than place the Lone Ranger's life and identity in jeopardy; the other one was the Ranger's white stallion Silver towards whom he displayed an affection he never showed any woman. The battle cry "Hi-Yo, Silver!" became the Lone Ranger's familiar trademark. (Tonto also had a recognizable mount, the paint Scout who was to Silver what he himself was to the Lone Ranger). In the middle Forties, following the fashion of the radio plays, there was introduced into the strip a teen-age companion to the Lone Ranger, his nephew Dan Reid, Jr., son of slain Captain Dan Reid, and future father of Britt Reid, the Green Hornet. Such is the stuff of mythologies!

Unlike such series as *King* and *Red Ryder* (which will be discussed later) plot and situations were subordinate to the Lone Ranger characterization. There were few genuinely gripping stories in *The Lone*

Charles Flanders, *The Lone Ranger*. Flanders is the artist most often associated with *The Lone Ranger*, which he drew from 1939 until its demise in 1971. © King Features Syndicate.

Ranger (one such occured in 1942 when a crooked businessman hired a circus freak named "the Skeleton" to close down a rival's mine by spreading terror among the workers). Usually there would be a stagecoach robbery, a bank holdup, or a string of cattle rustlings which the Lone Ranger would be called in to solve. There were also a number of stories involving defrauded widows, victimized orphans (mostly young girls) and wronged ranch-owners. Bankers were often villains, hiring gunmen to drive out cattlemen or sheep-raisers in order to foreclose on their loans and take over their land.

One familiar plot situation was to have the Lone Ranger accused (wrongly, of course) of some crime, and the masked avenger then would set out to find the real culprit (often a pillar of the community). In the course of his adventures, the Lone Ranger often came close to getting himself killed, or (worse yet!) to having his identity revealed. No outlaw, however, lived long enough to lift the mask off the face of the Western nemesis of crime. At the end of each episode the triumphant Lone Ranger would ride off on his horse, leaving behind him one of his silver bullets, as the symbolic trace of his passage.

The drawing of backgrounds had never been Flanders's forte, and the scenery in *The Lone Ranger* was one of the barest ever to appear in any newspaper strip Western: often a cluster of trees, a few mesquites, or a faraway mountain range were all there was to mark the location. A sense of place was therefore never achieved. The familiar landmarks of the Western *locus,* the deep gorges, craggy passes, mine tunnels, cattle towns, were indicated rather than delineated; they looked more like sets than real locations. *The Lone Ranger* always had the strange look of a storyboard for a grade-B Western movie; the real thing somehow always eluded the artist. The secondary characters all looked interchangeable and, more often than not, could be told apart only by the shape of their Stetsons or the color of their shirts.

The greatest popularity of the *Lone Ranger* strip came in the Forties, when Flanders reached his peak. Then erosion set in, as Flanders did less and less of the work, due to a serious drinking problem. Tom Gill, who was drawing the comic book version at the time, often came over to ghost the newspaper strip as well. Despite some imaginative writing by Paul Newman (who had succeeded Bob Green, who himself had replaced Fran Striker) the strip soon lost its following, and it was finally killed off by the syndicate in December 1971. A year or so later Flanders died in Palma-de-Mallorca where he had retired.

At the time of its demise, *The Lone Ranger* had been

appearing in newspapers for over 33 years, the longest run of any Western comic strip. Its longevity cannot be attributed to either remarkable story-telling or superior draftsmanship, although it was a reasonably well-done strip for the better half of its career. A good deal of its appeal, of course, lay with the title character's ambiguous role, a characterization so artfully contrived by Striker that it has resisted countless debunkings, spoofs and satires. But this is only part of the answer; the popularity of *The Lone Ranger* also stemmed from the resiliency of the Western myth itself. Plodding as they often were, the strip's plot elements fitted the tried-and-true conventions of the genre better then any of the competition. The writers did not try to overload their stories with psychological insights or philosophical speculations, they hemmed close to their theme. In this respect *The Lone Ranger* is probably the most representative of all American Western strips.

Fred Harman, or the pen that won the West

The comics' most important contribution to the Western mythos came, however, not from comic strip adaptations of already existing Western novels or serials, nor from the reflected glory of established Western authors, but from original stories specifically tailored to the comic strip idiom by an inspired journeyman artist named Fred Harman.

Fred Harman was born in 1902 in St. Joseph, Missouri, but grew up on his father's ranch in Colorado. After going through a variety of odd jobs, he decided to become a cartoonist. One of his first cartooning jobs was at a Kansas City advertising agency where he worked alongside his brother Hugh and another fledgling artist, Walt Disney. Moving to the West Coast, Harman created his first comic strip, *Bronc Peeler*, in 1934, a cowboy feature which he syndicated himself to a handful of newspapers in the West.

Bronc Peeler was a red-haired, callow ranch hand

Fred Harman, *Bronc Peeler*. Harman's red-haired cowboy in one of his usual scrapes. © Fred Harman.

who chanced upon the most unlikely adventures in the early days of the strip. He later aged by a few years overnight and acquired additional wisdom. Like most newspaper strip cowboys he ranged far and wide from his New Mexico base of operations in the company of Coyote Pete, his grizzled, somewhat befuddled sidekick. The action was set in contemporary times and Bronc more than once demonstrated that he was as expert at driving cars or flying planes as at riding horses. While some of the plots were quite conventional—involving cattle rustlers, crooked lawyers, and bank robbers—others were quite original. At one point, for example, Bronc was recruited by the FBI and the Mexican secret police to uncover a sinister organization bent on causing trouble on both sides of the Rio Grande by means of a deadly virus ("the red plague"). On another occasion Bronc and Pete discovered the lost Valley of the Aztecs, where the king's lovely daughter, Princess Moonbeam, inevitably fell in love with the carrot-topped hero and saved him and his companion from death at the hands of the wrathful Aztecs. At the conclusion of each of his exploits Bronc would always come back to his blonde, effervescent sweetheart, the long-suffering Babs.

After a few years Bronc acquired a new companion, an Indian boy named Little Beaver, in hopes of attracting a juvenile readership, but to no avail. *Bronc Peeler* folded in 1938, in spite of Harman's appealing, if rough-hewn, graphic style, and his minutious depictions of horses, cattle and Western scenery. Along with the *Bronc Peeler* Sunday page, Harman had also drawn a panel describing Western life and lore, *On the Range*, in which he indulged his penchant for didacticism, a trait that he would never lose in the course of his long career.

After the demise of *Bronc Peeler* Harman went East in the hope of finding work with one of the major newspaper syndicates. There he unsuccessfully tried out for *King of the Royal Mounted* and was about to head back home in bitter disappointment when Stephen Slesinger noticed his work and asked him to do a new cowboy feature for NEA Service. Harman simply plucked out his red-haired hero and his little Indian companion from his earlier creation and just threw them into new surroundings. Thus was *Red Ryder* born (the name—concocted by Slesinger—may have been inspired by the 1934 Buck Jones Western, *The Red Rider*).

The first *Red Ryder* page (November 6, 1938) must have set some record for narrative speed, even among the fast-moving adventure strips of the Thirties. In the course of the episode, Red (a) witnessed the fatal accident of Chief Beaver, (b) adopted his ten-year old

Fred Harman, *Red Ryder*. Red Ryder and his little Indian sidekick, Little Beaver, experienced a long and adventurous career that spanned three decades, two newspaper syndicates and a vast number of comic books not to mention twenty-two movies!
© NEA Service.

son, Little Beaver, (c) chanced upon a stagecoach hold-up, and (d) breezily determined to intervene—all in the space of eight panels! Harman, however, soon realized that such a breakneck pace was self-defeating and left no room for motivation or characterization. Wisely he adopted a more leisurely, even slightly detached, tone, while in no way sacrificing the necessary elements of action, suspense and derring-do. By the time the daily version of the feature rolled around in March 1939, *Red Ryder* was already in possession of all the characteristics that were to make it the champion of Western strips.

Of particular importance to the popularity of the strip was the authentic flavor of time and place that Harman was able to convey. The period—the 1890's, after the last of the Indian wars, but before the advent of the automobile—and the setting—the little town of Rimrock, in southwestern Colorado, at the foot of the San Juan Mountains, in the Blanco Basin—looked just right. Harman knew the region well. He had been raised there and later bought a ranch in Pagosa Springs, which we can imagine as being not too far removed from Rimrock. And he showed his meticulous passion for detail in many slight but interesting touches: Red Ryder, for instance, wears a flat-topped Stetson, typical of this semi-desertic area, and uses a Mexican saddle and stirrups adorned with tapaderos, all of which denote the strong Mexican influence in this part of the country.

The locale is also depicted with an almost archaelogical authenticity. The mining towns are pictured in all their rough-and-tumble rambunctiousness; the Mexican settlements are little more than adobe shantytowns; the ranch houses are rendered with gruff simplicity and no Hollywood glamor; and the Indian pueblos are drawn with almost photographic precision and without glossing over the squalor. Most impressive of all is the formidable presence of the Rocky Mountains, whose peaks and gorges tower over the pathetic goings-on among the men below.

In these surroundings Red emerges as one of the most unconventional of Western heroes. While his innate sense of justice drives him into some of his adventures, he can also be guided by more pragmatic motives, like tracking down a clever con-man in order to get back the thousand dollars he had been swindled out of, or joining a traveling circus to pay for some unexpected expenses. He had also been known to hire out his gun on occasion. "There are people who need me," he once declared on just such an assignment, judiciously adding, "and I'm bound to make a nice heap of money." He remains an impenitent bachelor, while keeping an appreciative eye out for the ladies—blonde-tressed, demure schoolmarms, fiery Mexican señoritas, wayward Indian princesses. Red makes no distinction of race, color or creed when it comes to romance. At any rate why should he marry? As Red himself once stated, he already has a family: his aunt, "the Duchess," a strong-willed, no-nonsense matriarch who helps Red manage his ranch, and his adopted son, Little Beaver.

Little Beaver, next to Red the most important character in the strip, is a Navaho Indian (the detail is important). Contrary to what some have asserted, Little Beaver's costume is correct and typical of his tribe: hair hanging loose, with a simple strip of cloth around the forehead, loin cloth and hip-high chaps. His language, however, is the kind of pidgin English favored by Hollywood hacks. "Him gettum plenty bad, Red Ryder!" A boy of unusual resourcefulness and pluck, Little Beaver would often get Red out of some tight spot, as in the episode in which he triggers a horse stampede to divert the attention of the outlaws who hold Red prisoner, and liberates the cowboy in the ensuing confusion.

If characterization, attention to detail, the slightest touch of pathos, and a penchant for wry humor are the hallmarks of *Red Ryder*, action remains the keynote of the strip, as befits a good Western of the old school. With its muddy, unpaved streets, shaky houses and run-down general store, Rimrock, for some unexplained reason, proves an irresistible magnet for outlaws of every stripe and description. Those desperadoes would have before long taken over the town (whose lonely defender is the cantankerous, ineffective sheriff Newt) had it not been for Red Ryder. Armed with his trusted .45 Colt revolver and Winchester rifle, Red could face any opponent. In the course of his adventures our hero has known some scary experiences; hung by the neck, his feet precariously resting on a shaky board; left to drown in a caved-in mine tunnel; closeted in a dark room with a rattlesnake. He has also been shot through various parts of his body, had

Fred Harman, *Red Ryder*.
© McNaught Syndicate.

his leg broken, been blinded with acid, and left spread-eagled under the scorching desert sun.

Whatever the hardships, however, Red has pursued his quarry with the relentless determination of the true Western hero. Along with the garden-variety crop of evil-doers plying the Old West, Red's enemies have included a whole slew of off-beat villains, such as the sinister gambler and hired assassin Ace Hanlon; Banjo Bill the music-loving killer who kept a gun concealed in his instrument; Donna Ringo the seductive leader of a gang of train robbers; not to mention a roving band of circus freaks working their depredations out of a traveling tent show. There were smaller fry, too, like the thieving twins, Oliver and Bolivar, and the incorrigible con-man, Buckskin. Around those characters and hundreds more, Fred Harman and his scriptwriters (chief among them was the talented Russ Winterbotham) wove tales filled with excitement and action, suspense and humor.

Fred Harman, *Red Ryder's Corral of Western Lingo*. Harman was much given to didacticism, and in his *Corral of Western Lingo* he endeavored to acquaint his readers with the finer points of cowboy practice and jargon. © Fred Harman.

In the Forties *Red Ryder* had become the most popular of Western strips by far. It was adapted into comic books (more of this in a later chapter), and brought to the screen; it was also voted "favorite comic strip" by the Boys' Clubs of America. Harman drew the strip in his forceful style, and with greater technical proficiency than he had shown in his earlier *Bronc Peeler*. *Red Ryder* could not compete in quality of draftsmanship with such outstanding creations as *Flash Gordon* or *Tarzan*, but it had a glow of its own, and displayed a virile line made of an odd mixture of awkwardness and concision. The Sunday feature was often accompanied by an educational panel called *Red Ryder's Corral of Western Lingo* in which Harman indulged his weakness for grammar-school pedagogics.

From the end of the Forties on, Harman grew more and more tired of the strip, and came increasingly to rely on "ghosts" who included, at one time or other, Edmond Good, Jim Gary, and the already mentioned John Wade Hampton. In 1960 Harman made his retirement from the strip official. "Many people have asked why I would give up the successful *Red Ryder* comic strip for the uncertain rewards of a Western painter," he later mused. "First of all, I quit the easy returns of commercial art and struggled five years to market *Red Ryder* because of my love of the West and, naturally, the large income from a syndicated comic strip. I had always painted, and in 1960, when my son and his family were successful on their own and the years were ticking by, I swapped saddles for the permanent satisfaction of trying always to do something better . . ." *Red Ryder* lingered a while longer under the inept pen of Bob McLeod, finally to disappear in the late Sixties—an ignominious end to this once-proud comic strip.

Red Ryder was the last Western comic strip of any note to come out of the Thirties. It also encapsulated all the virtues and weaknesses of the genre, in its breezy self-assurance, relentless action, and endless string of incidents and perils.

The fearless Forties

The Forties marked the heyday of the Western newspaper strip. Not only were the creations of the preceding decade—*King of the Mounties*, *Red Ryder*, *The Lone Ranger*, et al.—running very strong at the time, but new features were continuously added to the roster of comic-page horse-operas. None of the newcomers were to duplicate the success and popularity of the old Westerns, but a few of them are of more than passing interest.

The first Western to see the light of print in the Forties was *Gene Autry Rides!* Gene Autry had owed his success to an incredible Western-cum-science-fiction movie serial entitled *Phantom Empire*, the first (and only) singing Western set 25,000 feet underground. A shrewd businessman, Autry started merchandising himself, and one of his lesser efforts in the field was the aforementioned feature which came out as a Sunday half-page in the summer of 1940.

Gerald Geraghty and Till Goodan, *Gene Autry Rides!* Gene Autry did not enjoy as successful a career in newspapers as he did in films, probably because the singing cowboy could not sing in his strips. © Gene Autry.

THE EARTH RIDERS JOIN IN THE STRANGE ROUND-UP

Ray Bailey, *Vesta West and Her Horse "Traveler."* Vesta West, a piquant brunette, was one of the few heroines of Western strips. © Chicago Tribune-New York News Syndicate.

Written by Gerald Geraghty and drawn by Till Goodan, *Gene Autry Rides!* was a laughable enterprise which seemed doomed from the start. Goodan's graphic style was stiff and mannered, and Geraghty's prose at times unintelligible. The first story was a loose adaptation of *Phantom Empire*, and had Autry shuttling manically back and forth between his ranch and the underground kingdom of Murania. The goings-on looked even more ludicrous in cold print than they had on film five years earlier. More alarums and excursions followed as Autry, his elderly sidekick Frosty, and his horse Champion rescued ranchers threatened with foreclosure, mine owners stalked by foreign agents, not to mention an assorted bevy of damsels in distress. Autry's screen popularity did not rub off on the strip (of course his main asset—his singing—was sorely lacking), and Gene Autry stopped riding the comic pages in a matter of a few years.

In August 1941 veteran James Swinnerton (who had temporarily discontinued his *Little Jimmy*) tried his hand at a straight Western. A tabloid page titled *Rocky Mason, Government Marshal*, it had a run of less than a year. The first episode introduced Rocky Mason riding into town and taking on the local Mr. Big. The story involved a series of highway hold-ups masterminded by a mysterious boss-man (no mystery as to who the mastermind was, however). As much as one wishes to say only kind words about the work of one of the great comic strip pioneers, it must be conceded that *Rocky Mason* was not one of Swinnerton's best efforts. The drawing was too cartoony for a straight shoot-em-up, and Swinnerton's old-fashioned page layout did not allow for visual excitement. As it is the strip remains an oddity in the artist's career.

At about the same time that *Rocky Mason* was being terminated (1942) Ray Bailey started *Vesta West* for the News-Tribune Syndicate. *Vesta West and Her Horse "Traveler"* (to give the feature its full name) was a Western with a different touch: its protagonist was not a hero, but a heroine, a brunette bombshell drawn in the best pin-up tradition. With the help of her brawny

James Swinnerton, *Rocky Mason, Government Marshal*. *Rocky Mason* was Swinnerton's short-lived attempt at drawing a straight Western strip. © King Features Syndicate.

Burne Hogarth, *Drago.* Drago was a South American Western graced with some of the author's most superlative artwork. © Burne Hogarth.

assistant Grits who took care of most of the rough stuff, Vesta handled herself remarkably well in her encounters with highway agents, land grabbers and claim jumpers. The strip was drawn in a loose, very pleasant style, with each character sharply defined. This early blow for Women's Lib did not last long, however; *Vesta West* folded in 1944, with Ray Bailey going on to draw *Bruce Gentry* for the Hall Syndicate in 1945.

As it turned out, that same syndicate was a little later to hire Burne Hogarth (who had just quit *Tarzan*) to do a new Sunday page for them: this was *Drago*. While some purists may quibble that *Drago* was not strictly a Western because the action was set in Argentina, it certainly stayed close to the conventions and accouterments of the genre. (Actually many Argentine readers of the strip bitterly complained that *Drago* gave a totally unreal image of their country—a fact which later stunned Hogarth who had done a great deal of preliminary research.)

His first adventure found Drago (a more youthful-looking version of Tarzan) and his comic sidekick Tabasco pitted against the sinister Baron Zodiac, a Nazi war criminal who had set up shop in the pampas. Zodiac, with the help of some local fascist types, was readying a wild scheme designed to trigger a third world war (a special worry of the times). Drago would, of course, foil the conspirators' nefarious machinations and blow up Zodiac's hideaway. The action was conveyed in a weird blend of old and new, with wild horse rides alternating with car chases, submarine landings and helicopter escapes. The second episode came closer to stock Western plotting. In an effort to clear his father, Drago would don cape and mask, in the tradition of Zorro, and expose the miscreants trying to discredit the family name.

Of greater importance than the hackneyed plots, however, were Hogarth's incredible feats of draftsmanship and stunning layouts. The backgrounds, settings and landscapes were all depicted with a dazzling virtuosity of color and line, and the opulence of the costumes and sets was almost too overwhelming. Never had any comic strip Western displayed such a wealth of images: *Drago* looked like a Hollywood spectacular accidentally lost in the midst of a grubby bunch of grade-B pictures. Despite its undeniable artistry and its popularity with the readers, *Drago* was dropped by the syndicate late in 1946. The reason given by the syndicate was that *Drago* duplicated the action of *Bruce Gentry* (which was also set in South America) but it is more likely that the editors felt ill at ease with Hogarth's reckless display of virtuosity. (At least this is the artist's side of the story, and it rings true insofar as Hogarth was a better-known and more highly regarded artist than Bailey, even at the time.)

Western creations still kept coming. In 1949 Dan Spiegle, fresh out of art school, was hired by William Boyd, the star of the famed *Hopalong Cassidy* movie series, to draw a comic strip based on his screen characterization. Distributed by the Los Angeles Mirror Syndicate, the strip debuted on January 4, 1950.

The character depicted by Spiegle was very close in appearance and comportment to the "Hoppy" of the movies. The first story was written by Dan Grayson, one of Boyd's finance managers, and by Spiegle, but later a writer named Royal King Cole (sic) was hired. Cole contributed many interesting narratives, often taking Hoppy out of his usual locale, and putting him into strange surroundings, such as the San Francisco waterfront, and even Australia (where Hoppy was taken after being shanghaied aboard a contraband ship).

Spiegle's draftsmanship kept improving with each passing episode, as he gradually abandoned the rough-hewn linework of his early drawings for a more subtle rendering based on a mix of Craftint and dry brush techniques. The effect became especially striking after distribution of the strip had been taken over by King Features in 1951. Around that time Spiegle also deepened his utilization of color (in the Sundays) thus adding a further dimension of drama. In the early Fifties *Hopalong Cassidy* was undoubtedly one of the best-looking of Western comic strips. The stories, however, did not keep pace with the strip's advances in draftsmanship, and were being more and more diluted on pressure from the syndicate. In the mid-Fifties, when the hue-and-cry against violence in the comics reached its crescendo, King Features quietly decided to drop the strip. (At its peak in 1952 *Hopalong Cassidy* had a list of over 200 newspapers.) The comic art career of the durable black-shirted cowboy was not to be ended so cavalierly, however, and we shall find him riding again in the comic books.

As was mentioned earlier, Buffalo Bill is probably the most widely-known figure of the legendary West, and inevitably a number of features based on his fictional exploits were to see print over the years in the United States, and even more frequently abroad. All of the American confections were of short duration, and all of them of little interest, with the exception of Bill Meagher's version in the early Fifties. While not an outstanding artist, Meagher nevertheless succeeded in breathing some epic life into his short-lived creation (less than two years).

The longest-lasting Western strip born in the Forties

Dan Spiegle, *Hopalong Cassidy*. Spiegle contributed much to the legend of the movie Western star with his taut scripts and well-researched backgrounds. © King Features Syndicate.

Fred Meagher, *Buffalo Bill*. One of the many comic strip versions of the life of the fabled Indian scout, Meagher's was also one of the more pleasurable. © United Feature Syndicate.

turned out to be not an original creation but the revised version of Ferd Johnson's old *Texas Slim* (soon to be renamed *Texas Slim and Dirty Dalton*). Starting its second (or third) life in the comic-book sized supplement of the Chicago *Tribune* in March 1940, *Texas Slim* was to last until 1958. In the course of its reincarnation it displayed for the first time some real fireworks, as Johnson unfolded a number of suspenseful and action-packed narratives interspersed among the more familiar comic routines.

Finally let us mention the last Western to come out in the Forties (in December!), *Roy Rogers*, by Al McKimson.

The turn of the decade saw the high water mark of the Western comic strip. Indian-fighters and bronc-

NOTHING EVER DIES
(especially reader interest!)
IN "DEATHLESS VALLEY"

—mythical locale of a rootin', tootin', laugh-packed Western satire by Russ Stamm. Newspapers in major cities are holding regular readers and winning new ones with

....SCARLET and CHIPS

—a daily strip and Sunday color page featuring superb character drawing, fast-paced continuity, humorous dialogue. New episode starts Oct. 3. Wire for proofs today!

CHICAGO SUN-TIMES
Syndicate INC.
211 W. WACKER DR.

HARRY B. BAKER GENERAL MANAGER

Russ Stamm, *Scarlet and Chips.* © Chicago Sun-Times Syndicate.

"JED COOPER—American Scout"

FROM THE ADVENTURE-FILLED PAGES OF AMERICA'S PAST comes a great new Sunday color comic, relating the exploits of an intrepid young frontiersman among the Indians and assorted varmints of the early western wilderness . . . a tale of rugged action for every one of your readers. Ask to see sample proofs now.

CHICAGO TRIBUNE - NEW YORK NEWS *Syndicate* INC
M. SLOTT, Manager   NEWS BUILDING, New York 17   TRIBUNE TOWER, Chicago 11

Announcement for *Jed Cooper—American Scout.* © Chicago Tribune-New York News Syndicate.

busters came tumbling out of the newspaper pages in an endless and colorful cavalcade. Most of the newcomers, born in the feverish years 1949-51, proved short-lived, but a few should be noted here; these were conceived with high hopes and nurtured with affection, but met with an indifferent and uncaring public. Their unique flavor can best be conveyed in the claims made for them by their syndicates:

"Nothing ever dies (especially reader interest!) in 'Deathless Valley'—mythical locale of a rootin', tootin', laugh-packed Western satire by Russ Stamm. Newspapers in major cities are holding regular readers and winning new ones with *Scarlet and Chips*," the Chicago Sun-Times Syndicate proudly proclaimed in 1949.

In January 1950 the rival Chicago Tribune-New York News Syndicate came up with *Jed Cooper—American Scout*, which was trailered thus: "FROM THE ADVENTURE-FILLED PAGES OF AMERICA'S PAST comes a great new Sunday color comic, relating the exploits of an intrepid young frontiersman among the Indians and assorted varmints of the early western wilderness . . . a tale of rugged action for every one of your readers."

The Register and Tribune Syndicate touted its brand new *Laredo Crockett* with these words: "Here's the new action-packed strip that sizzles with six-shooters, fast horses and the real drama of Old Texas. It's by Bob Schoenke and exclusively for newspapers starting June 12 (1950)."

Bob Schoenke, *Laredo Crockett*. © Register and Tribune Syndicate.

Brand New
And Exclusively for Newspapers
LAREDO CROCKETT

. . . Here's the new action-packed strip that sizzles with six-shooters, fast horses and the real drama of Old Texas. It's by Bob Schoenke and exclusively for newspapers starting June 12.

Phone or Wire for Terms.

REGISTER AND TRIBUNE SYNDICATE
DES MOINES   **25 W. 45TH ST., NEW YORK**

Warren Tufts, *Casey Ruggles*. *Casey Ruggles* was a violent and realistic tale of the Western frontier, set in the time of the California gold rush. © United Feature Syndicate.

Fred Meagher's *Buffalo Bill* also received ecstatic treatment from its syndicate, United Feature, when it came out in July 1950: "Buffalo Bill! Every American, young and old, will thrill to the daring, dashing exploits of this famous Western hero! It's a fast-breaking, free-wheeling story! It's cowboys and Indians! It's BUFFALO BILL!"

The most ironic casualty of the period was *Bronc Saddler*, a modern-day Western introduced in January 1951. Written and drawn by brothers Del and Herb Rayburn, the feature received more lavish praise than the inconspicuous panel that Post-Hall Syndicate was offering at the same time, and which turned out to be *Dennis the Menace*. *Bronc Saddler* died ignominiously, while *Dennis* is still going strong, a telling commentary on the course of the American newspaper strip over the last 25 years, during which occurred a progressive switching of reader interest to TV Western (and action) series and away from adventure comics.

A time of turmoil

The Fifties opened on a hopeful—or at least complacent—note for Western comic strips: the horse-operas had just reached their peak in popularity and, because of the Westerns' long and established tradition of violence, seemed immune to the mounting attacks against action comics. The syndicates' admonition to artists and writers alike was: Stick to formula, don't rock the boat. One man, however, rebelled against these strictures and definantly engaged the Western on an independent and exciting new path.

The lone dissenter was Warren Tufts, born in California in 1925, who abandoned a successful radio career to create *Casey Ruggles*. Actually the strip started in 1949 but belongs absolutely to the Fifties (it was ahead of its time even then!) Subtitled "A Saga of the West," *Casey Ruggles* was set in the days of the California gold rush. Casey was an army sergeant serving with Fremont; after a brief interlude in the East, where he became involved with Lilli Lafitte, (daughter of fabled pirate Jean Lafitte) to the chagrin of his long-suffering fiancee, Chris, Casey went back to California. There he met with violence and skulduggery among the conflicting claims of Yankee gold prospectors, Spanish land holders, and dispossessed Indians. Tufts was especially sensitive to the plight of the red man, and one of the more attractive characters in the strip was Kit Fox, an Indian boy.

Casey Ruggles flew in the face of all the genteel conventions of comic strip Westerns. It was filled with sweat, blood and tears, as Tufts graphically depicted the back-breaking labor, treacherous dealing and dreary existence that went into the making of the Western frontier. Occurences of rape, torture and murder were related matter-of-factly, and no hold was barred in this grim tale of human courage, resiliency, cunning and greed. The public, reared on a diet of conventional Western stories, soon started protesting, and *Casey Ruggles* was finally dropped by the syndicate in 1954.

After a half-hearted attempt at a science-fiction spoof called *The Lone Spaceman*, Tufts went back to the Western motif with *Lance*, a full-color, full-size Sunday page which he started syndicating himself, with the help of his father, beginning in June 1955.

Lance StLorne, the titular hero, was a second-lieutenant with the U.S. First Dragoons, headquartered at Fort Leavenworth, Kansas, in the 1840's. Lance's outfit was assigned the policing of the territories west of the Missouri, and the task led them into a series of bloody encounters with the Sioux. Like *Casey Ruggles*, *Lance* was an historically-oriented strip, and Tufts described the Indian campaigns with a documentary accuracy, even introducing historical figures such as the fabled Indian scout, Kit Carson, into the narratives. The story-telling was highly realistic: blood flowed copiously, and sexual relationships were described with unusual candor.

Lance, after a fast start, (picking up about 100 newspapers, many of them in the larger cities) began to falter after a couple of years. Tufts cut back the feature to half-page, then third-page size. In spite of his last-ditch efforts *Lance* went steadily down, until its creator ultimately abandoned it in 1960. Any hope of a realistic, hard-bitten portrayal of the West in newspaper strips went down along with it.

In the early Fifties King Features decided (again) to launch another old-fashioned Western. Again they turned to a well-known property, in this case *The Cisco Kid* (based on O. Henry's story "The Caballero's Way") which had already known countless retellings on the screen. The writing was entrusted to staffer Rod Reed, while the syndicate reached all the way to Argentina to come up with a suitable artist, the talented José-Luis Salinas. *The Cisco Kid* first appeared on January 15, 1951.

Like his *compadre* Zorro, the Cisco Kid was a Mexican righter of wrongs, an indefatigable fighter against the crime and corruption afflicting the New Mexico territories at the turn of the century. Impeccably attired in a richly-embroidered black outfit and wearing a huge sombrero, he has become one of the legendary figures of the American West. In company of his comic sidekick, the pot-bellied and crafty Pancho, his rides often took him far from his usual field of operations.

BROKEN NOSE HAS DONE THE IMPOSSIBLE, MOUNTING A THOUSAND WARRIORS TO THE ENEMY'S REAR. GLORY IS WITHIN HIS GRASP...AND SO HE LAUGHS WHEN THREE OF THE ENEMY CHARGE FURIOUSLY FROM HIDING!

HE LAYS DOWN A BARRAGE OF ARROWS, THE HAPLESS SOLDIERS DIVE FOR COVER...AND THE FOLLOWERS OF BROKEN NOSE JOIN HIM IN RAUCOUS LAUGHTER. WAR FEVER BOILS AFRESH... THE MULTITUDE SHRIEKS FOR THE KILL!

A THOUSAND TO THREE...STICKS AND BONE AGAINST ROCK AND POWDER..... AN UNEVEN BATTLE.

IN AN INSTANT TONS OF ROCK DESTROY THE NARROW TRAIL...DELIGHT TURNS TO STARK TERROR... THE ENTIRE INDIAN ARMY IS STOPPED COLD!

...THEN, QUICKLY, ONE AFTER ANOTHER, THE CRUDE GRENADES PITCH INTO THE RANKS... AND BROKEN NOSE, COMPLETELY STUNNED, WATCHES HIS SPLENDID ARMY BACK INTO A HOPELESS PILEUP.....

THE ACTION CONSUMES LESS THAN A MINUTE WHEN LANCE SIGNALS A HALT. PANDEMONIUM IS COMPLETE...THE "WAR" IS OVER.

BROKEN NOSE HAS WITNESSED A NIGHTMARE FROM WHICH HE CAN NEVER RECOVER. HE CHOOSES A DOUBTFUL FUTURE AS A PRISONER OF THE WHITES TO NO FUTURE AMONG HIS OWN KIND.....

Warren Tufts, *Lance*. Tufts followed *Casey Ruggles* with the equally tumultuous *Lance*, a bloody saga of the Indian wars. © Warren Tufts.

The first story involved the Cisco Kid in an entertaining story of graft, land speculation, and underhanded dealings, with a clever twist at the end. It also introduced the character of Lucy Baker, a beautiful blonde suffragette type, that no man, not even the sinister Judge Hook, the villain of the piece, could silence.

Other adventures found the Kid and Pancho pitted against a hooded extortionist calling himself "the Black Ghost," fighting the redoubtable outlaw Big Bull, and bringing to heel a gang of train robbers led by the notorious Red Lariat. One of the most entertaining narratives came in 1959 when our hero confronted the gun-toting, tough-talking Babe Puma, a kind of Annie Oakley as adept at karate as at broncho-riding or marksmanship. At first rivals, Babe and Cisco would join forces to outwit a trio of swindlers trying to put the "Babe Puma Wild West Carnival" out of business.

The Cisco Kid enjoyed interesting story-lines, good characterization, and superlative artwork from the pen of Salinas. The magnificent scenery and open spaces of the West were lyrically evoked in Salinas's black-and-white compositions (there never was a Sunday version). In spite of all its qualities the strip failed to hold its public, and it was discontinued in August 1968. Its demise was much lamented by all aficionados of the genre.

In the Fifties the Associated Press introduced the first (and only) Western strip they were ever to distribute. Called *Young Ray Bold* it was an odd mixture of off-beat plotting and old-fashioned drawing from Fran Matera, a cartoonist best known for his brief tenure on Coulton Waugh's *Dickie Dare*. The strip went nowhere and was dropped after a couple of years. (Coulton Waugh himself tried his hand at a Western strip around the same time; titled *Tall Boy*, it was a tender and attractive feature, but unfortunately it did not find any outlet.)

Created by Stan Lynde for the News-Tribune Syndicate in 1958, *Rick O'Shay* occupies a unique position among Western strips, midway between humor and adventure. At first Lynde had placed the action in modern times, which gave him a chance at some innocent fun based on anachronistic situations. Later (in 1964) he wisely turned the clock back to the last years of the 19th century, and the strip has assumed its definitive aspect ever since.

The setting of the feature is the former ghost town of Conniption where a number of off-beat characters have elected to domicile themselves over the years: First there was Deuces Wilde, the gambler who proclaimed himself mayor of the town and appointed his likable partner Rick O'Shay as marshal. They were later joined by Hipshot Percussion, the gunslinger;

Rod Reed and José-Luis Salinas, *The Cisco Kid*. O'Henry's Western rogue came alive again in 1951, thanks to the talent and skill of his Argentine comic strip illustrator, the incomparable José-Luis Salinas. © King Features Syndicate.

Fran Matera, *Young Ray Bold.* A Western with a modern locale, *Ray Bold* displayed some pleasant graphic qualities. © AP Newsfeatures.

Gaye Abandon, the saloon singer and Rick's heart throb; Basil Metabolism, M.D.; the Mexican cowpoke Manual Labor, and others.

Alternating them with gag situations, Stan Lynde has been able to develop hard-hitting, fast-paced, realistic narratives, especially in the dailies. The hero of these suspenseful tales is most often the rugged, hard-boiled Hipshot, who in recent times has been given more and more of the scenes. In recognition of the fact, the strip became known as *Rick O'Shay and Hipshot.*

When Lynde created *Rick O'Shay*, the popularity of the Western strip was already on the wane. Since the demise of the *Lone Ranger* in 1971, *Rick O'Shay* remains the only Western with any sizable following; it is also the most authentic since the early *Red Ryder.* The artist (who owns a 160-acre ranch near Billings, Montana) is particularly skillful in his depiction of horses, cattle, and Western landscapes and settings, all of which he does with documentary precision. That he still feels obliged to mix slapstick with action is testimony, however, of the low state in which straight Western adventure has now fallen.

The end of the trail

Following *Rick O'Shay*, newspaper readers had to wait seven years before any new feature set in the West would come their way; and when it finally arrived it turned out to be not the usual cowboy and Indian shoot'em-up, not even a gentle spoof, but a full-fledged satire of the genre. Thomas K. Ryan, a commercial artist, was bored with his work and he sought refuge from it in Western literature; from his readings came *Tumbleweeds*, a strip which endeavored to combine, in the artist's own words, "the Old West with a hip approach."

The action is set in the ramshackle frontier town of Grimy Gulch, presided over by the irascible Judge Frump, ineptly assisted by the sheriff and his dull-witted deputy, Knuckles. The town's other worthy citi-

Coulton Waugh, *Tall Boy*. Despite its obvious charm and appeal, *Tall Boy* remains unpublished. © Coulton Waugh.

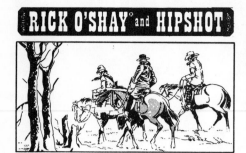

Stan Lynde, *Rick O'Shay*. Occupying a unique position, midway between humor and adventure, *Rick O'Shay* has managed to maintain a consistently good story-line and a high level of graphic excellence. © Chicago Tribune-New York News Syndicate.

zens form a hilarious gallery of Western stereotypes; there can be found Sopwell, the inveterate saloon drunk; Ace, the sharp-dealing, fast-shuffling gambler; Claude Clay the undertaker ("You plug 'em, we plant 'em") and his lugubrious assistant Wimble; the visiting outlaw Snake Eye ("At the earliest age I became associated with shady characters . . . my parents."), not to mention a benumbed Indian scout and Gus, the cowboy that can't shoot straight.

In this rundown burg there also lives Tumbleweeds, the most inept, slowest-moving, slowest-witted cowboy that ever plied the West. Mounted on his anaemic and faint-hearted nag grandiosely named Epic (who in turn had succeeded the equally rickety Blossom) Tumbleweeds takes great pains to avoid any undue entanglements, as well as any work that may come his way. He would live a happy and carefree existence, basking in the obscurity of his talents, were it not for the persistent Hildegard Hamhocker, the town spinster, who constantly tries to force her slobbering affections on the reluctant cowpoke. Hildegard, whose favorite reading matter is the "husband-hunters' manual," is perhaps the most endearing character in the cast, and her endless rounds of pursuing, counteracted by Tumbleweeds's no less determined dodging, constitute one of the highlights of the strip.

An especially funny sideshow is provided by the neighboring tribe of comic-opera Indians in constant (as well as futile) war with the hapless garrison of Fort Ridiculous, commanded by the feckless Colonel Fluster. ("Colonel, this means war. Tomorrow we attack at dawn!" "At dawn! . . and me miss my breakfast?")

Originally Ryan had intended *Tumbleweeds* to be a gag strip, but later he went more and more deeply into humorous continuity, while keeping a sharp eye on the 30-odd characters that populated the strip.. His graphic style is simple, even basic, harking back to the caricatural line of the early cartoonists. His creation is a good example of the modern brand of irreverent humor.

What *Tumbleweeds* did to the myth of the rugged West, *Redeye* was to do to the legend of the noble Indian. Gordon Bess created the strip in 1967 and it has been going strong ever since.

Redeye is the slightly befuddled sachem of a no less soft-headed tribe of Indians who live on the borderline of white civilization (or what passes for such) in a state of half-war, half-peace. Grouped around him are some of the most incompetent, faint-hearted and querulous braves ever assembled around a wigwam—always ready to run the opposite way when the sachem orders a charge, or to get drunk on smuggled firewater. Tanglefoot in particular is an albatross around the sachem's neck: not only can't he tell a herd of stomping buffaloes from an oncoming train, but his insistence in wanting to marry Tawnee, the sachem's lovely daughter, is enough to drive Redeye into homicidal fury. Nor are these the sachem's only trials: he is poisoned by his wife's cooking, badgered by his

T.K. Ryan, *Tumbleweeds*. Ryan has written an uproarious satire of the Old West, based on a keen sense of characterization and a flair for outrageous humor. © King Features Syndicate.

Bess Gordon, *Redeye*. This rollicking saga of a tribe of dumbfounded Indians is one of the best of the modern humor strips. © King Features Syndicate.

young son Pokey, outsmarted by his medicine man, and constantly thwarted in his dreams of military glory by his cowardly mustang, Loco.

The screwball situations of *Redeye* are blended with the author's first-hand knowledge of the West (Bess lives in Idaho), and scenery, animals and customs are depicted with a deft, if satirical, hand.

Rowland Wilson, *Noon*. © Chicago Tribune-New York News Syndicate.

The success of the parodic Western incited other cartoonists to follow suit. Also in 1967 *Playboy* cartoonist Rowland Wilson brought out *Noon*, about an ineffectual and loud-mouthed cowboy named Noon Ringle. Noon's harebrained exploits pitted him against a variety of adversaries whom he usually overcame with a mixture of breeziness and dumb luck. Wilson's scattershot approach did not suit the requirements of Western satire which ask for close focusing on some instantly recognizable trait or foible. The characters were all too broadly drawn for such a purpose, and the strip did not survive the decade.

The only noteworthy addition to the ranks of the Western to come out of the Seventies is *Catfish*, written by Gary Peterman and drawn by Rog Bollen, yet another entry in the "how the West was fun" contest (the strip started in 1973).

Gary Peterman and Rog Bollen, *Catfish*. *Catfish* is one of the latest entries in the flourishing dumb-cowboy sub-genre. © Chicago Tribune-New York News Syndicate.

Catfish is a sometime Pony Express rider, sometime Indian scout for the U.S. cavalry. Mounted on his stallion Molasses he can be counted on to deliver the mail (usually mangled in the rough ride) with his accustomed alacrity, or to lead a party of cavalrymen straight in the wrong direction. Other protagonists in the strip are the foul-tempered Major Mustard and the sissified Lieutenant Faircatch, the leaders of an outlandish army outfit at war with Chief Sitting Eagle's tribe of Chickadee Indians.

A blatant attempt to cash in on the popularity of *Tumbleweeds*, *Catfish* is not even half as funny. The gags are belabored, and the situations often absurd where they should have been satirical. Worse of all is Bollen's slapdash rendition of characters and situations, and his obvious lack of familiarity with things Western.

Perhaps better than any writer could do, *Catfish's* sorry example graphically summarizes the plight of the Western in the second half of the Seventies. With the exception of *Rick O'Shay*, there is no longer any nationally syndicated newspaper strip of Western adventure. At a time when Westerns exhibit a healthy and vigorous renaissance in comic books as well as in foreign comic publications, the trend can only be attributed to short-sightedness and lack of imagination on the part of syndicate editors, and on artistic sterility on the part of syndicate cartoonists, an aging and enfeebled breed.

CHAPTER TWO
THE WESTERN COMIC BOOK

© Hugo Pratt

The comic book Westerns constitute a veritable paper jungle in which it is very easy for the unwary reader to get lost. There are literally hundreds and hundreds of different titles, some of which disappear to reappear a number of years later, others that keep the same title but completely change their cast of characters, yet others that seem to wander aimlessly from one company to another like some sun-crazed prospector in search of the elusive El Dorado. Comic book companies are compulsive name-changers, and they have often muddied the waters further by changing the names of their publications at the drop of a hat, sometimes even perversely changing their numbering system without warning or justification.

This is, I believe, the first methodical attempt at bringing some order to the chaos of Western comic books, as well as the first serious inquiry into this hitherto little-researched field of popular literature. We will try to follow the most successful, famous or noteworthy Western features through all their sometimes bewildering transformations, reincarnations and permutations.

The first draft (1937-1940)

The first Western stories to appear between comic book covers were reprints of newspaper strips (with minor alterations to suit the new format) regularly featured in such publications as *Tip Top Comics*, *Popular Comics* and *King Comics*. Original material soon started cropping up; among the earliest recorded comic book Westerns, one of the more noteworthy (because of its author) was *Lightnin' and the Lone Rider* which Jack Kirby drew under the pseudonym of Lance Kirby for *Famous Funnies* in 1937. Another early Western creation by Kirby was *Wilton of the West* which appeared in *Jumbo Comics*, starting with issue No. 4 (December 1938).

The early comic books tried to present their readers with a variety of material, and each title included at least one Western adventure series. *Whiz Comics* (which starred the original *Captain Marvel*) had *Golden Arrow*, about a Western super-hero type raised in the wilderness, one of whose artists was Al Carreño. *Flash Comics* presented *The Whip*, a reasonable facsimile of the Zorro legend, by John Wentworth and George Storm; even *Action Comics* No. 1 in which *Superman* was first introduced contained a Western story by Bernard Baily, *Tex Thompson* (later changed to a super-hero strip, as *Mr. America*). There were also *The Masked Rider* and *The Masked Ranger*, both obviously derived from the *Lone Ranger* syndrome. Yet specialization had already set in, and comic books devoted exclusively to Western adventure soon sprouted all over the place. *Western Action Thrillers*, which lasted only one issue, sported *Buffalo Bill* and *The Texas Kid* as early as 1937; Centaur Comics published two Western comic books: *Cowboy Comics* and *Star Rangers*, both similarly short-lived (1937-38). Obviously if the Western comic book was to survive as a separate entity more exciting heroes had to be found. Again the comic book publishers turned to the newspaper page.

The first long-lasting Western success in the comic book field turned out to be *Red Ryder*, which first appeared in September 1940. The first two issues of *Red Ryder Comics* were published by Hawley Publications, but with issue No. 3 (August 1941) the title passed to Dell where it remained until the last issue (No. 151 of April 1957) by which time it was known as *Red Ryder Ranch Comics*.

WITH LIGHTNING SPEED BRADDOCK GOES FOR HIS GUN.

BUT BEFORE HE CAN SQUEEZE THE TRIGGER A GOLDEN ARROW KNOCKS THE REVOLVER OUT OF HIS HAND.

THROW UP YOUR HANDS ALL OF YOU!

UNSEEN BY GOLDEN ARROW BRAND BRADDOCK PRESSES A SECRET BUTTON SUMMONING HIS COWBOY HENCHMEN.

IF YOU WEREN'T AN OLD MAN, BRADDOCK, I'D SETTLE WITH YOU MYSELF FOR MURDERING MY FATHER. BUT I'LL LET THE LAW HANDLE THAT.

TUCKING THE STOLEN FORMULA INTO HIS JACKET, GOLDEN ARROW PREPARES TO LEAVE.

JUST THEN BRADDOCK'S COWBOYS ARRIVE.

QUICKLY GOLDEN ARROW RAISES HIS BOW, AIMS—

Golden Arrow. The anonymous *Golden Arrow* was one among the many short-lived Western tales that were common in the pages of early comic books. © Fawcett Publications.

John Wentworth and George Storm, *The Whip*. A Zorro-like masked avenger, the Whip put in a short appearance in *Flash Comics*. © DC Comics, Inc.

Edmond Good (?), *Red Ryder*. Fred Harman's red-haired newspaper strip hero had become so popular by the early Forties that he sported his own long-lasting comic book, unfortunately "ghosted" by other hands. © Dell Publications.

The first issue of *Red Ryder Comics* reprinted episodes from the newspaper strip, along with some decidedly non-Western features such as *Dan Dunn*, *Captain Easy*, and *Alley Oop*. After a few years, however, the red-topped cowboy and his cohorts pushed the other comic strip heroes out of the book. Soon the newspaper stories ran out, and original material had to be introduced. By the late Forties the comic book was made up entirely of original stories. While consistently signed "Fred Harman" the comic book version was in fact written and drawn by a variety of hands, most of them anonymous. In addition to Harman's already mentioned assistants, John Wade Hampton and Edmond Good, the team also included Al McKimson and Dick Calkins who, upon his departure in a huff from *Buck Rogers* in 1947, had moved west and was presently to become *Red Ryder's* chief scribe, with the help of his son, Dick Calkins, Jr.

Coasting on the popularity of the newspaper strip and later of the movies and radio program, the comic book enjoyed great success among the young readers. While the stories used the same cast of characters as the strip, they did not, however, have the same ring of authenticity. Aiming at a juvenile audience they resorted to the well-worn clichés of the Saturday matinee shoot'em-ups—bank robberies, stage hold-ups, nightriders, etc. The restrictive episode length, usually from eight to ten comic book pages, also precluded the kind of story and character developments that were the hallmark of the newspaper feature.

Red Ryder was no longer the tough-minded, down-to-earth character of his early adventures, but just another prairie justice-fighter, only distinguished by his red shirt, and the "R" displayed on his chaps. No longer saddled with secondary concerns (such as making a living) he could roam at will over plain and mountain, bringing outlaws to justice, returning stolen gold to grateful prospectors, and defending widows and orphans from the greedy designs of shady lawyers. Gone, too, was Red's earthy speech, to be

Little Beaver. Even Red's little Indian companion was to enjoy his own strip. © Dell Publications.

replaced by what can only be called Western gothic ("Jumpin' catfish! it was plumb careless of me!")

Too often Red would share the spotlight with his aunt who had her own feature in the book, titled *Auntie Duchess*. She proved to be as tough as her nephew: in one episode she foiled an Apache raid single-handedly. "All you women and kids," she would warn the startled townsmen, "get into the stone warehouse! *Pronto!* You men, get your guns . . ." Even more popular was the *Little Beaver* feature which starred the little Navaho Indian involved in a variety of entertaining scrapes. So popular did he become that from 1951 to 1953 Little Beaver had his own comic book.

True to his long tradition of didacticism Fred Harman presented his readers with at least two long-running vignettes of Western life. One, simply entitled *Cowboys*, detailed in a friendly tone some of the history of the West and depicted daily ranch life accompanied by a full-page illustration, usually drawn by Harman himself. The other, *Wigwam Ways*, was a genuine comic strip, spread over two or three pages, that presented with great honesty and uncontrived warmth of feeling, the ways, customs and traditions of the old Indian tribes of North America.

Another early comic book cowboy was Tom Mix; his adventures, however, could not be found on newsstands for the price of a dime, but were mailed out free by the Ralston Purina Company to any young reader who sent in two boxtops of Ralston cereal. The Ralston people had had great success with the Tom Mix advertising newspaper strip as well as with the radio program, and they thought that the comic book might duplicate those.

Wigwam Ways. Also appearing in *Red Ryder Comics*, this was a feature presenting with honesty the ways, customs and traditions of the old Indian tribes of North America. © Dell Publications.

LONG BEFORE THE WHITE MAN CAME TO AMERICA, MANY INDIAN TRIBES PLAYED A WILD, ROUGH FORM OF "FOOTBALL"!

Fred Meagher, *Tom Mix*. The *Tom Mix
Comics* could be obtained free in exchange
for two Ralston Purina boxtops. © Ralston
Company.

Jesse Marsh, *Gene Autry*. Gene Autry was another movie cowboy who made it big in comic books. © Dell Publishing Co.

In addition to the adventures of the title hero, *Tom Mix Comics* contained a feature called *Jane at Dream Castle* (a distinct imitation of *Little Nemo*) as well as games, tricks and premium toy offers. Tom Mix's first comic book adventure involved the screen cowboy and Tony, his "wonder horse," in the mystery of Ghost Canyon. Later he was to put down a Mexican revolution and go on to discover the lost treasure of the Toltecs. (A favorite pastime among all cowboys of the era was the search for long-vanished tribes and their treasures.) His adventures got more and more fantastic as Tom battled the mad scientist known as the Cobra, tangled with a sea serpent, and saved Fort Knox from an audacious raid on its gold bullion.

In his exploits Tom Mix was assisted by the Straight Shooters (a holdover from the radio series) which comprised his young ward, Jane, the Old Wrangler and the black cook Wash. The Straight Shooters were more often than not a hindrance rather than a help, but their devotion to their leader was inspiring.

A month after the release of the first issue of *Tom Mix Comics* (September 1940) the real-life Tom Mix was killed in a car crash, but the comic books never even hinted at the accident; apparently Mix had by then entered the field of mythology. In 1942 the comic book was retitled *Tom Mix Commando Comics*, while the hero and his cohorts took on with zest the task of fighting Japanese submarines, Nazi raiders, and other enemies of the American way of life, in the patriotic spirit of the times. In November of the year, however, the comic book was discontinued, following the cancellation of the radio show. The radio program was later reinstated, but *Tom Mix Comics* never saw the light of print again, at least as a premium publication.

Tom Mix was one of the better comic book Westerns. The stories—all of them original—were written by editors Stan Schendel and Ray Bouvert, the artwork was supplied by the excellent, albeit underrated, Fred Meagher who did a splendid job of pencilling, and the inking was done by Bill Allison.

Other comic books were from time to time to present the adventures of Tom Mix, usually with poor results. The only other publication worth noting here is Fawcett's *Tom Mix Western* which was, from 1948 to 1953, the prolongation in comic book form of the familiar yarns of the radio series.

Comic book cowboys of the Forties

For the best part of the decade the Western gunslingers had rough going in the comic books. The superheroes had taken over the field in ever-increasing and ever-more clamoring numbers. The coming of the war also worked in favor of the costume-wearing league: Superman, Spy Smasher, Captain America, and the rest of the super-powered bunch seemed a better match for the Nazis and the Japanese than were the gun-toting, bronc-riding denizens of the range. However slow the pace, creation continued none the less, with quality making up for lost quantity.

In 1941 Gene Autry made the transition from newspaper page to comic book. The singing cowboy was to know a long, if checkered, career in the medium. He first appeared in his own book, *Gene Autry Comics*, published by Fawcett until 1943, then taken over by Dell only to be dropped early the next year. He then fitfully rode across some of the issues of Dell's all-purpose *Four-Color Comics*, sandwiched between such non-heroic characters as Felix the Cat and Porky Pig. This undignified exile ended in 1946 when Dell reinstated the monthly *Gene Autry Comics* which lasted till 1959, by which time it was known as *Gene Autry and Champion*. Champion was of course Gene's horse, who had a few comic books of his own in the Four-Color series. To make the record even murkier Gene Autry also starred in a number of comic book premiums and giveaways not sold on newsstands, but given out free as either straight promotion, or in exchange of proof of purchase of the advertised product for such companies as Pillsbury, Tim Stores, and K.K. Publications.

Startlingly enough, the comic book stories, while avowedly aimed at a juvenile audience, were better than those in the newspaper strip, and the artwork, uneven as it was, had its bright spots, with such solid craftsmen as Peter Alvarado, Al McKimson and Nat Edson (fresh out of ghosting the *Tim Tyler's Luck* newspaper strip for Lyman Young). By far the best artist on the series was Jesse Marsh who managed to convey in *Gene Autry* the same feeling of spaciousness and vitality as in his later *Tarzan*.

Autry, in the meantime, had been succeeded at Fawcett by another film cowboy, the black-suited Hopalong Cassidy. Actually Hoppy had appeared in comic books even earlier, in issue No. 33 of *Master Comics* (November 1942), but he now enjoyed his own book. Hopalong Cassidy was to stay with Fawcett from 1943 to 1954, when he passed over to National Periodicals, finally ending his comic book career in 1959. In the meantime Hoppy, like Tom Mix and Autry before him, helped peddle a line of wholesome products, in this case Bond bread and Grape Nuts cereal, to the youngsters of America by means of the customary giveaways.

Dan Spiegle, *Hopalong Cassidy*. © The Mirror Syndicate

The stories in the *Hopalong Cassidy* comic books were of the traditional shoot'em-up and lasso'em-in variety. Despite Captain America's glowing endorsement on the cover of the first issue ("Hopalong's my choice for rootin' tootin' Wild West action"), the goings-on were rather predictable, with Hoppy displaying solid, but unspectacular, qualities of horsemanship and pugnaciousness. The art in these comic books also lacked the kind of punch that only a first-rate draftsman could deliver. The artists were adequate at best, with Ralph Carlson perhaps the most consistent. The comic book's longevity seems due more to the Hopalong Cassidy movies and later to the TV program than to any quality of its own. In fact the character proved so popular that Fawcett put out a companion publication, *Bill Boyd Western*, with plots adapted from the movie series; it lasted for 23 issues, from 1950 to 1952.

With Hopalong Cassidy and Gene Autry already on the scene could Roy Rogers be far behind? The answer came in 1944 when Roy and Trigger made their appearance in that same Four-Color series that had helped launch its rivals. The results must have looked promising to the publishers, for *Roy Rogers Comics* hit the newsstands as a full-fledged publication in January 1948.

Roy Rogers. © Dell Publishing Co.

Dan Spiegle, *Roy Rogers*. With Autry
already on the scene could Roy Rogers be
far behind? Of course not . . . © Dell
Publishing Co.

The comic books, which always featured Roy Rogers in full regalia on its covers (sometimes with Trigger, less often with Dale Evans) closely followed the plots and themes of the Rogers movies, minus the musical interludes, of course. Roy Rogers would usually ride into town only to be confronted by trouble of some sort (a rancher unjustly accused of murder, a holdup in progress) and, with the help of his faithful stallion Trigger, he would bring the criminals to justice. There always were some good action scenes, with long panoramic panels, and good page layout. The dialogue and characterization never rose over grammar-school compositon ("Blazes! He tricked us!" would exclaim one disgruntled cattle rustler outwitted by Rogers's quick thinking.) There was an amusing back-up feature, called *Chuckwagon Charley's Tales*, in which the title character would recount the real or imagined exploits of youngsters in the days of the wild frontier.

Chuckwagon Charley's Tales. Chuckwagon Charley was a back-up for Roy Rogers, and he provided some much-needed comic relief. © Dell Publishing Co.

Roy Rogers Comics became Roy Rogers and Trigger in 1955, and the stories became more and more childish; by the time of its demise in 1961 the level of plotting and characterization was so low that it could only have been aimed at the nursery-school set.

If the writing of Roy Rogers was generally under par, it enjoyed good and even sometimes excellent art by Peter Alvarado, Al McKimson, John Buscema and Nat Edson. Particularly praiseworthy were those stories illustrated by Alex Toth and by Russ Manning who was called in at the end of the run in one last effort to stop the comic book's unrelenting decline.

The Roy Rogers comic books were successful enough in the Fifties to warrant two spin-off publications, Roy Rogers' Trigger (1951-55) and Dale Evans (1953-59). They both proved undistinguished although Dale Evans sported some pleasant artwork by Nick Cardy. Roy Rogers also appeared in a couple of giveaways (Roy Rogers and the Man From Dodge City, for Dodge cars, notably).

Paul Newman and Tom Gill, *The Lone Ranger*. The comic book version of the Lone Ranger's exploits was entertaining and well handled. © Lone Ranger, Inc.

O. Henry's lovable frontier rogue, the Cisco Kid, underwent his first comic art incarnation in 1944, when comic book artist Bernard Baily decided to go into business for himself. *Cisco Kid Comics* lasted for only three issues, despite Baily's tight supervision of the scripts, and good artwork by John Giunta. The Cisco Kid was to surface again in the Fifties in another series of comic books released by Dell from 1950 to 1958. It tried to cash in on the success of both the TV series and the newspaper strip, but only succeeded in turning out a batch of lame Western stories, poorly written and indifferently illustrated.

As a curiosity we should note here a comic book intermittently published by Magazine Enterprises under the name of *Cowboys 'n' Injuns*, and later *Cowboys and Indians*; it was a kiddie variation on the Western theme, with a blond tousle-haired little boy of five as hero, and an assortment of animals characters, Indian papooses, and bearded old-timers in the supporting roles. The comic book's career extended from 1946 to 1952.

Another short-lived creation of the Forties was *Western Adventure Comics* which lasted for six issues from 1947 to 1949. It featured the exploits of Sheriff Sal, and some interesting plotting.

Paul Newman and Tom Gill, *The Lone Ranger.* © Lone Ranger, Inc.

This period of the Forties can be said to have come to a close with the appearance on the newsstands, late in 1947, of *The Lone Ranger* comic book (the issue was actually dated January-February, 1948, but, as is customary in the comic book business, it was released for sale some months before that date). The Lone Ranger, of course, was no stranger to the medium; reprints of the newspaper strip had appeared as early as 1939 in such publications as *King Comics*, *Ace Comics* and the Four-Color series, but his graduation to a comic book of his own signalled the start of a new era.

The first 37 issues of the new comic book consisted of reprints of the Charles Flanders daily strips and Sunday pages, published in no particular chronological (or logical) order. With issue No. 38 original stories began to appear, written by Paul Newman (no relation to the actor). Newman was very careful not to tamper with the Lone Ranger legend, and he carefully incorporated all the characters of both the newspaper strip and the radio program into his stories. While often hampered by the format of the tales, usually no more than ten or eleven pages in length, Newman contributed some interesting twists to the masked avenger's saga. Under his tutelage the Lone Ranger became a kind of all-purpose troubleshooter, master sleuth and unofficial guardian of the peace on the frontier. One of Newman's ploys was to whet the appetite of the readers with a short illustrated synopsis of the stories on the inside front cover: "When Dan Reid is mistaken for a runaway boy, he suddenly finds himself the object of a big search and the key to a robbery plot . . ." or "A gang of robbers striking lonely prospectors in the High Rockies are stopped when they try to hit a peddler's wagon - but they escape . . ."

Newman milked every plot and cliché from the Western thesaurus. North and south, from the Canadian border to the Painted Desert, his masked rider and his companions, Tonto and newphew Dan Reid, proved the scourge of every law-breaker that ever rode the West. The stories were always interesting, sometimes gripping, and they earned Newman the scriptwriter's spot on the *Lone Ranger* newspaper strip, after Striker departed. Most of the artwork in the comic book was contributed by Tom Gill, a solid draftsman. The drawings and compositons held few surprises, but they were enjoyable: Gill was especially good at handling horse rides and shooting scenes, two of the staples of the Western genre, and the two situations most often and most prominently displayed in the comic book version.

The Dell *Lone Ranger* came to an end in 1962. This was not to be the end of the masked rider's career in comic books, however. Gold Key picked up the title in 1962 and has been continuing it, with major and minor interruptions, up to the present time. There also was a spin-off titled *The Lone Ranger's Famous Horse Hi-Yo Silver* (quite a mouthful), which Dell put out from 1952 to 1956; and the Lone Ranger, like most other famous comic book cowboys, was also featured in a series of giveaways and premiums (touting breakfast cereal, milk, and ice-cream, among other products).

STAN LEE PRESENTS
KID COLT OUTLAW

"the RETURN of IRON MASK!"

YOU FIRST MET THE AMAZING *IRON MASK* IN KID COLT #110! THE KID'S BATTLE WITH THIS SEEMINGLY UNBEATABLE FOE WAS ONE OF THE TOUGHEST FIGHTS OF HIS LIFE! BUT NOW, *IRON MASK* RETURNS -- MORE DANGEROUS, MORE INVINCIBLE THAN EVER! SO SIT BACK, RELAX, AND PREPARE TO READ ONE OF THE MOST EXCITING WESTERN ADVENTURES YOU'VE EVER SEEN -- A MOVIE-LENGTH KID COLT SPECTACULAR IN THE MARVELOUS MARVEL MANNER...

ORIGINALLY PRESENTED IN KID COLT #114

| WRITTEN BY: | DRAWN BY: | LETTERED BY: |
| STAN LEE | JACK KELLER | ART SIMEK |

Stan Lee and Jack Keller, *Kid Colt, Outlaw.*
Kid Colt is one of the more entertaining cowboy features to come out of the Forties.
© Marvel Comics Group.

The golden age of the Western (1948-1954)

In the years following the end of World War II the hitherto invulnerable super-heroes started going into a slump; readership declined markedly and even the mighty Superman was adversely affected. Comic book publishers started frantically to scramble for a new (yet proven) formula, as comic book publishers are always wont to do in times of crisis. Some turned to crime and horror comics (with results that were to prove disastrous for the industry); others, better inspired, decided to go back to the established and respectable Western format, a genre that made the violence deemed necessary for the sale of comic books more palatable in the eyes of concerned parents (the young readers did not have to be sold). Western titles in this period grew to gigantic numbers: I have counted more than one hundred titles, but there are many others which have doubtless escaped my notice. It would be an exercise in futility to list them all here, most of those being very short-lived and/or without

Stan Lee and Dick Ayers, *Two-Gun Kid*. The Two-Gun Kid was another one of the Western heroes created by Stan Lee. © Marvel Comics Group.

any merit, but there remain more than a few that are worthy of discussion.

One of the more entertaining of the cowboy features of the time was *Kid Colt, Outlaw*, started as *Kid Colt, Hero of the West*, in 1948. A written introduction was later tacked on each opening story to explain to the readers the origins of Kid Colt, and how he happened to become an outlaw. It read:

"The Legend of Kid Colt . . . Years ago, Kid Colt killed an outlaw in self-defense! But, being young and foolish, he fled, instead of staying to stand trial! Since then, he has spent his life trying to atone for his mistake!"

Of course the theme of the reformed outlaw is at least as old as pioneer Western movie actor and director William S. Hart's *The Taking of Luke McVane* of 1914, but it still remains effective. Much of the Kid's time was spent eluding by-the-book sheriffs and tangling with bounty hunters or would-be malefactors who were forever trying to pin their own crimes on the pure-hearted outlaw. Later on in the stories the fair-haired, youthful-looking gunslinger would make at least tacit peace with the authorities, the better to turn his attention to crime-fighting on a large scale.

In the course of his career Kid Colt met a number of outlandish criminals, among them the Iron Mask, one of his most constant foes, who donned a suit of armor under his Western garb, in order to make himself impervious to bullet fire. In one episode the Kid shot him in the arms (unwittingly left unprotected). When the Iron Mask made his return (after a jailbreak) with an improved model he then lured him into a creek, where the Mask's armor got rigid with rust, rendering its wearer helpless!

Kid Colt was scripted by some of the best writers in the business, including Stan Lee, and was graced with pleasant and at times superlative artwork from such luminaries as Jack Kirby, Reed Crandall, Al Williamson, Gray Morrow and Joe Maneely. The book was discontinued in 1968, and revived the next year, chiefly in the form of reprints of older stories.

The publishers of *Kid Colt*, Atlas, now Marvel, Comics, also put out *Two-Gun Kid* that same year, 1948. Starring what the blurbs proclaimed was "the wildest cowboy in the wild West," it also had good stories, excellent artwork by Kirby, Williamson, Crandall, as well as by Jack Davis, Bill Everett and Bob Powell. Interrupted in 1949, *Two-Gun Kid* again surfaced in 1953, and is still running today, chiefly as a reprint comic book.

Atlas came up with at least two more Western titles of interest in that fateful year, 1948. The first was *Wild West* (retitled *Wild Western* later in the year), and con-

Mort Meskin, *Wild Bill Pecos the Westerner.*
Excellent drawings and breakneck action
were the hallmark of this Western comic
book. © Lev Gleason.

sisted of stories featuring those two stalwarts, Two-Gun Kid and Kid Colt, as well as real-life figures of the old West, such as Annie Oakley and Wyatt Earp. *Wild Western* ended in 1957.

The second Atlas title was to know a parallel but much more colorful career. Started as *All-Western Winners* in 1948, it changed its name successively to *Western Winners* the next year, then to *Black Rider* (1950-55), before ending its long run in 1963 as *Gunsmoke Western.* In addition to the inevitable Two-Gun Kid and Kid Colt, the comic book also included *Black Rider,* the tale of a black-masked, black-attired avenger, in the mold of the Lone Ranger; there also was *Wyatt Earp,* billed as "pages of true tales from the life of the West's most famous peace officer." Stan Lee wrote many of the stories (some were narrated in the first person) in his unmistakable manner, with a powerful assist from artists Jack Kirby,

Doug Wildey, Jack Davis, Steve Ditko and Dick Ayers.

National Periodicals put out *Western Comics*, also in 1948. Some of the stories included *Pow Wow Smith, Indian Lawman; The Wyoming Kid; Rodeo Rick;* and, most interesting of all, *Nighthawk*, about yet another hooded figure of justice, by the name of Hannibal Hawkes, whose emblem, a hawk emblazoned on his shirtfront, spread terror in the hearts of prairie evildoers, much as National's Batman was already doing with Gotham City criminals. The comic book lasted until 1961.

Another 1948 creation of note was *Wild Bill Pecos the Westerner* which ran until 1951. The stories and the art were almost uniformly excellent, with vivid depictions

Nat Edson, *Tim Tyler Cowboy*. Tim Tyler was plucked out of the African wilds to fight outlaws of the Wild West. © King Features Syndicate.

of gunfights, stampedes and conflagrations. The action was relentless, even brutal, with such ruthless villains as the leader of an outlaw gang known simply as "the undertaker," and the colorful Ma Joad, all of them brought to heel in the end by Wild Bill Pecos, "famed two-gun marshal of Tombstone." As a back-up feature the book included *Lobo* (not to be confused with Marvel's later strip of the same name), the tale of a white boy raised by Cherokee Indians. Mort Meskin and Bernard Krigstein were the most notable art contributors to *Wild Bill Pecos*.

In that prolific year 1948 Western comic books just seemed to tumble over one another as far as the wide horizon. Tim Tyler came out of the African jungles to face some Western perils in *Tim Tyler Cowboy*. Unfortunately the flavor, mood and quality of the *Tim Tyler* newspaper strip did not transfer well to the new locale, and the book was discontinued in 1950, in spite of some good artwork by Nat Edson whose name was for the first time signed to the drawings.

Fred Guardineer, *The Durango Kid*. This comic book was loosely based on Charles Starrett's popular series of movie Westerns. © Magazine Enterprises.

Frank Frazetta, *White Indian*. This feature owed its success to Frazetta's inimitable style of detailed anatomy. © Magazine Enterprises.

The year 1949 proved hardly less productive, and one of the memorable comic books of the year was *The Durango Kid*, loosely based on Charles Starrett's popular series of movie Westerns. The hero was heir to the long tradition of anonymous avengers, who used not a mask, but a black neckerchief to cover his face and keep his identity secret. Along with his sidekick, Old Mort, he helped the maintenance of law and order on the prairies. There was also a "Durango Kid's Western Dictionary," but the main attraction of the comic book was Frank Frazetta's back-up feature, *White Indian*.

Drawn in "Fritz" Frazetta's inimitable style of detailed anatomy—both male and female—and striking composition, it told of the valorous deeds of Dan

Brand, "the white Indian," and his companion Tipi, in their fight against the British during the War of Independence. The stories were later reprinted in a series of *White Indian* comic books (1953-55) and are now considered classics. The *Durango Kid* comic book also came to an end in 1955.

And still they came . . . Lev Gleason, notorious for his crime comics, put out *Black Diamond Western* (formerly *Desperado*), about yet another masked rider who fought outlaws, marauding Apache bands, claim jumpers and a mysterious criminal mastermind known as the Scorpion. The comic book was on the whole undistinguished, with only the wildly parodic *Bing Bang Buster* by Basil Wolverton as its · redeeming grace; it lasted from 1949 to 1956.

Avon Publications tried its luck with *Wild Bill Hickok*, one more in the long list of comic book borrowings from the historical West. It was an entertaining, if altogether spurious, account of the life and times of the famed lawman, with wild stories of Indian uprisings, legal chicanery and over-the-border raids in the free-wheeling days that followed the Civil War. The artwork, well rendered, at times suspenseful, and certainly never dull, was provided by such old hands as E. R. Kinstler and Mort Meskin. Begun in 1949, *Wild Bill Hickok* ended its career in 1955.

Wild Bill's trusted friend of the old Pony Express days, William "Buffalo Bill" Cody, was also accorded the honor of his own comic book. In fact he had at least *four* comic books bearing his name, a record that should have gratified the old showman in his grave. The first recorded instance is that of *Buffalo Bill's Picture Stories* turned out by the pulp publishers Street and Smith. (It is interesting to note that the same Street and Smith had published an illustrated book of the same title as far back as 1909!) Lasting for only two issues in 1949, the title is chiefly remembered for the artwork of Bob Powell and Doug Wildey whose first comic book assignment it happened to be. This was followed by *Cody of the Pony Express* (1950-51), another version bearing the same title (later changed to *Buffalo Bill Cody*) in 1955-56, and even a *Buffalo Bill Jr.* (1956-59)

Another child of this fecund year 1949 was *Rocky Lane Western*, whose chief interest resided in its plotline. Rocky Lane was a U.S. marshal acting as an undercover agent in the days of the old West, in order to expose dishonest sheriffs, crooked Indian agents, and subversive groups of vigilantes. The reader would surely have recognized the underlying theme of the TV series, *The Wild Wild West*. Rocky Lane's horse, Black Jack, was given the honor of his own comic book named (what else?) *Rocky Lane's Black Jack*, first is-

Jack Keller, *Apache Kid.* "Kids" of all denominations and of all ethnic groups are very popular among comic book Western heroes. © Marvel Comics Group.

sued in 1957. Both *Rocky Lane* and *Black Jack* were discontinued in November 1959.

Before closing the book (no pun intended) on the decade of the Forties mention must be made of *Prize Western Comics*, whose first issue also came out in 1949. The publication presented a number of excellent Western stories, written with both pathos and restraint by John Severin, and illustrated by Al Williamson, Will Elder and Mort Meskin. The best feature in the book was *American Eagle*, drawn by Severin himself, and characterized by comic book scholar Joe Brancatelli as "one of the few serious, relatively unbiased handlings of the American Indian in comic books." Despite its high level of draftsmanship and story-telling, *Prize Western* failed to catch the enduring attention of its mainly juvenile audience, and it was discontinued in 1956.

In 1950 a Western with a different touch appeared as a sub-series in Magazine Enterprises' "A-1" collection: *Ghost Rider*. The Ghost Rider was a Western avenger whose spectral appearance (along with that of his horse) struck terror in the hearts of his superstitious enemies. The series, whose author remains unknown, was drawn in a bold and striking style by Dick Ayers. The Ghost Rider also made appearances in other titles such as *Tim Holt Comics*, *The Best of the West*, *Red Mask* and *Bobby Benson's B-Bar-B Riders* until the demise of the "A-1" series in 1955.

In 1967 writer Stan Lee decided to revive *Ghost Rider*, and Dick Ayers was again chosen to illustrate; unfortunately the new series lasted for only seven issues. It should not be confused with the current *Ghost Rider* comic book about a preternatural motorcyclist.

To further confuse matters the original Ghost Rider stories were reprinted in 1974-75 under the title of *Night Rider!*

The theme of the mysterious justice-fighter marched on and on, with some novel twists. Aloysius Kane, for instance, was a mild-mannered rancher who, at the sight of a wrong being commited, would turn into the dreaded Apache Kid, complete with feather headband and war paint. *Apache Kid* appeared as a distinct comic book from 1950 to 1956, then for one more year in *Western Gunfighters*. *Apache Kid* was also featured in *Two-Gun Western*, drawn by John Buscema and Steve Ditko, among others. It could also be found in the form of reprints in the new, revised *Western Gunfighters*, where it shared the space with reprints of *Western Kid*, *Gun-Slinger*, and others, from 1970 to 1975.

In 1950 Fawcett came out with a comic book anthologizing practically every one of its Western heroes. It was called *Six-Gun Heroes*, and boasted the exploits of Rocky Lane, Hopalong Cassidy, Smiley

Burnette and Lash LaRue, among others. When Fawcett discontinued its comic book operation in 1954, the title was taken over by Charlton, where it remained until it was discontinued in 1965. It offered standard Western fare, enlivened by a few good stories, and by the late appearance of Tom Mix in issue No. 24.

A horse opera of a different color, *Tomahawk* also first appeared in that year 1950, published by National Periodicals. *Tomahawk* had the distinction of being one of the very few long-lasting Westerns not set in the second half of the 19th century. It related the adventures of an enterprising group of rangers working behind British lines for General Washington. The hardy little band was composed of the fair-haired, coonskin-capped leader, Tomahawk; his lieutenant, the herculean Big Anvil; the sharp-shooting Wildcat; and the youthful Brass Buttons.

Some of the group's exploits were predictable: ambushing British troops, raiding redcoat headquarters, fighting off Indian enemies, etc. Others were more outlandish. On one occasion Tomahawk and his companions were pitted in a struggle to the last against an Indian raider mounting a giant wasp! The writing was pithy and straightforward with such old hands as Ed Herron and Bill Finger at the typewriter, but the illustrations varied widely in quality, from the excellence of a Frazetta all the way down to the mediocrity of a Fred Ray. In 1970 the comic book went on to become *Son of Tomahawk*, jumping a few decades in time, but the facelift did not improve sales, and the title was dropped in 1973.

Publishers, looking any which way for new titles, had to reach deeper and deeper into Western history. One, Charlton, came up with *Jim Bowie* from 1953 to 1957. The book told of the mythical exploits of this frontiersman against the Mexicans and his last stand

Fred Ray, *Tomahawk*. *Tomahawk* was an early Western set in the times of the War of Independence. © DC Comics, Inc.

at the Alamo. The Mexicans were made to look like sap-headed louts, with no allowance for the other side of the coin.

Don Heck, *Old Scout*. *Old Scout* was the main attraction of a comic book called *Death Valley*. © Charlton Comics.

That same year, however, Charlton also introduced the much superior, if largely ignored, *Death Valley*, which lasted for only nine issues into 1955. Its main attraction was *Old Scout*, well handled by Don Heck, which purported to be the reminiscences of an aging Cavalry scout during the days of the Indian wars. The story was told in the first person and it was effective. *Death Valley* also contained a couple of back-up features, the indifferent *Six-Gun Larson*, and the intriguing *Bill Folers*. Bill Folers was a rope-throwing troubleshooter who looked like a dead ringer for Will Rogers, down to the homespun philosophizing. After having brought a gang of road agents to book, he would sententiously intone for the benefit, no doubt, of his young readers: "Everybody gets what's comin' to 'em in this world, an' no more . . . no less!"

From Billy the Kid to the Sundance Kid there has always been a goodly number of "Kids" in Western history. Because of the youthful connotation that such a name carries there has been an even greater number of Kids in Western comic book history; and no fewer than three of them saw the light of publication in the year 1954.

The first to arrive on the scene (in August) was *The Ringo Kid,* perhaps inspired by the character played by John Wayne in *Stagecoach.* The comic book protagonist was, however, a lot younger looking and far more neatly dressed, in his dark blue outfit and red neckerchief, than his movie counterpart. The Ringo Kid's mission was never too well defined, but he seemed to have some secret ties with the authorities, be they the commandant of Fort Cheyenne or the local sheriff, in order to keep outlaws, gun-runners, hired killers, and other "owlhoots" in check. One of his most constant concerns was to avert any trouble with the Indians—no easy task with all kinds of despicable characters running around the West trying to inflame the red man with rhetoric and whisky. In these circumstances, the Ringo Kid's blood brother, the Cheyenne brave Dull Knife, was always of assistance.

The Ringo Kid. One more Western "Kid." © Marvel Comics Group.

The Ringo Kid was one comic book Western with a good idea of what it was about. One story lead-in read: "Progress came slowly to the West! It came in painful spurts accompanied by violence and disorder as a sprawling territory was tamed! Order emerged from chaos by the rule of the gun, and two of these guns belonged to the Ringo Kid . . ." The stories did not always live up to their promises, but they were readable and the writers did not write down to their public. Most of the artwork was done by Joe Maneely and Joe Sinnott, with occasional contributions by Al Williamson. *The Ringo Kid* ended its too brief career in 1957, but it was revived in 1970, mostly as a reprint comic book.

Doug Wildey, *The Outlaw Kid*. And still they came . . . © Marvel Comics Group.

The Outlaw Kid appeared a month later (September). The Kid was that old stand-by, the masked avenger with a dual identity. In this case he was "easy-going, shy Lance Temple." The stories were at best serviceable, but Doug Wildey's artwork, oddly derived from Frank Godwin's style of penmanship, was first-rate. As Joe Brancatelli writes: "Wildey's photographic art style, based heavily on his morgue of picture clippings, made *The Outlaw Kid* a popular feature."

"Sure," Ben Bolt replies, "Just to scare bad hombres who respect a lawman only because they may think he's a killer like themselves! I never killed a man in my life!"

The book also benefited from the penwork of men like Reed Crandall, Russell Heath, Bob Powell and the ubiquitous Al Williamson. It unfortunately disappeared in 1957.

Before passing to the next period in Western comic book history mention should be made of a number of publications with such wonderfully descriptive titles as *Blazing West* (which featured a heroine called "Buffalo Belle!"), *Western Frontier*, *Saddle Justice* (E.C. Publications' one try at Western adventure), *Crack Western* (with stories by Reed Crandall), *Firehair*, *All-Star Western*, *Western Thrillers*, *Billy the Kid* (whose exploits were depicted by Williamson and Frazetta among others), *Badmen of the West* and *Masked Ranger* (about yet another Lone Ranger type).

All these publications saw the light of print in the short period from 1949 to 1954, as did two intriguing titles, both with a romantic angle aimed at a feminine public: *Cowboy Love* and *Cowboy Romances*. The latter lasted for only three issues in 1949-50; the former consisted of five issues, published sporadically between 1949 and 1955.

The Comics Code and its aftermath

Ever since their creation in the late 19th century the comics have been the object of countless attacks. Before World War I they had been accused of fostering a spirit of disrespect and insubordination among children by their glorification of cheeky, iconoclastic urchins like the Yellow Kid and the Katzenjammer Kids. After World War II the attacks increased in intensity, especially against comic books which were denounced by psychologists, pedagogues and demagogues as undermining the morals of youth. These charges culminated in 1954 with the publication of Dr. Fredric Wertham's book, *Seduction of the Innocent*, and the ensuing investigation into comic books conducted by the Senate Committee on the Judiciary chaired by Senator Estes Kefauver. Taking fright, the comic book publishers later that year established the Comics Code Authority, a self-regulating body which set forth a stringent set of standards limiting severely the depiction of crime and violence in the comic books.

The Code had a disastrous impact on most adventure comic books, but in a perverse way it helped sustain the popularity of the Western. Because of the traditional, almost ritual, depiction of Western violence, the genre was less emasculated by the Code

The Outlaw Kid ran from 1954 to 1957, before being revived in the form of a reprint comic book in 1970.

The third of our Kids, *The Western Kid*, arrived on the last month of the year. It was all about another clean-cut, right-thinking justice-fighter, always accompanied by his two "fighting pals," the horse Whirlwind and the dog Lightning. The story of *The Western Kid* is much the same as that of its two predecessors: born in 1954, gone by 1957, with reprints appearing from 1971-72.

John Romita, *The Western Kid.* © M
Comics G

The same eventful year 1954 saw the birth of the anthology-type *Western Outlaws*, which contained three or four short stories in comic form per issue. Some of the stories' titles will give the reader a hint of their contents: "Trail of the Owlhoot," "A Gunman in Town," "The Rio Kid Returns," "Thundering Colts." These tales were soberly written, as in the story titled "Twelve Notches".

In Pecos Village, Ben Bolt, the new sheriff, sports twelve notches on his gunhandle, and he outbluffs a passing outlaw without a shot being fired. To the sheriff who calls him a coward the bandit exclaims: "You got twelve notches on your gun, haven't you?"

Joe Gill and Pat Boyette, *Cheyenne Kid.* This comic book hero proved to be one of the more successful of Western "Kids." © Charlton Comics.

Larry Lieber, *Rawhide Kid.* © Marvel
Comics Group.

than the more objectionable crime, horror and super-hero comics. Westerns thrived in this second half of the decade, with new creations coming out in numbers almost equal to those of the preceding years.

The most popular figure of 1955, the year in which the Code took full effect, was unquestionably Davy Crockett, who had been given a big boost by the popular Walt Disney movie of that title, as well as by the hit song, *The Ballad of Davy Crockett*. The famed frontiersman and Alamo defender was starred in his own book, *Davy Crockett, Frontier Fighter*, published by Charlton from 1955 to 1957, and made numerous appearances in Dell's Four-Color series, where his adventures were drawn by Jesse Marsh. The character also enjoyed a brief period of fame in Europe at the time, with two separate versions drawn by Le Rallic and Martin Sièvre in France, and a third series created by Gianluigi Bonelli in Italy.

Some publishers reached even further back into Western history—all the way to Daniel Boone, the fabled frontier-fighter of the early days of the Republic, when the West was any territory across the Alleghenies. There were *The Legends of Daniel Boone*,

Stan Lee, *Matt Slade*. Matt Slade, gunslinger, was one more notable contribution made by Stan Lee to the Western genre. © Marvel Comics Group.

published by National from 1955 to 1957, *Exploits of Daniel Boone* (1956-57) released by Quality Comics, and Magazine Enterprises' laconically titled *Dan'l Boone;* unfortunately none was very distinguished.

A longer-lasting comic book of 1955 was Charlton's *Wild Frontier,* which featured one more version of the coonskin-hatted Davy Crockett in its first issues. The editors soon realized that Crockett was a drag on the market, and in issue No. 7 they introduced the character of Cheyenne Kid. As the name implied the hero had grown up among the Cheyenne Indians; he was later to become an Indian scout in the service of Colonel Mackenzie, commander of the fort at Sour Springs. His main task was to keep the peace among the Indian tribes of the plains, by solving their legitimate grievances, or thwarting plots forever being hatched by greedy gun-runners. To prevent an uprising among the Cheyennes the Kid even fought a man-to-man duel with the bellicose leader of the insurgents. Naturally, he won. The character soon became so popular that the comic book was retitled *Cheyenne Kid* in 1957, and lasted well into the Seventies.

During its 17-year run *Cheyenne Kid* boasted some notable illustrators; John Severin, Al Williamson and Angelo Torres chief among them.

The year 1955 also saw the comet-like passing of *Western Tales* (it died the next year), notable mainly for Joe Simon's and Jack Kirby's *Boy's Ranch* stories. This comic book also included *Jim Bowie,* and -what else?- *Davy Crockett.*

In 1955 writer/editor Stan Lee made a further contribution to the lore of the Western comic book with *Rawhide Kid.* As initially conceived by Lee, the Rawhide Kid was a ruthless gunslinger using both gun and bullwhip with brutal effectiveness. The violence had to be toned down, however, under the provisions of the Code and, within a year, the Rawhide Kid had abandoned his whip and his triggerman reputation to live the life of a rancher on a cattle spread near mythical Shotgun City. Along with his protégé, Kid Randy, the hero kept peace and order in the town, rounding up cattle rustlers and outlaws. The new format proved to be unsuccessful, and *Rawhide Kid* folded in 1957.

The title was revived in 1960, with Jack Kirby pencilling and Dick Ayers inking the drawings. The revamped version featured a totally different Rawhide Kid, an orphan named John Bart, adopted by retired Texas Ranger Ben Bart. The elder Bart taught Johnny his skills at fast drawing and marksmanship; and after Ben was gunned down by a gang of outlaws, Johnny avenged his father's death and thus became an outlaw himself under the name of Rawhide Kid. In

TEXAS RANGERS IN ACTION in Badland Friend

THIS WAS THE TEXAS BADLANDS... WHERE THE COMANCHEROS TRADED FIRE-ARMS TO THE RENEGADES AND OWL-HOOTERS...WHERE EVERY MAN'S HAND WAS AGAINST THE LAWMAN! IT WAS HERE THAT TEXAS RANGER RUDD FERRIL CAUGHT UP WITH THE MEN WHO HAD LOOTED THE CENTRALLIA BANK...

COME ON, BONES...FERRIL'S TOO GOOD WITH THAT HANDGUN! WE'LL PICK THE PLACE TUH PUT HIM DOWN!

Texas Rangers in Action. Claiming to be based on real cases out of the files of the Texas Rangers, this comic book put heavy emphasis on slam-bang action and fast-moving plot. © Charlton Comics.

the course of his wanderings the Rawhide Kid had several brushes with the law. He had to fight it out on numerous occasions with aspiring gunslingers itching to inherit the Kid's mantle, while at the same time atoning for his dark deeds by freeing some town from the grip of a gang of killers, or by saving a wagon train from marauding Apaches. One of the Kid's most deadly encounters occurred when he crossed paths with the bank-robbing gang of Ma Morgan and her three murderous sons; it ended with the wiping out of the entire family!

Among the artists who worked on *Rawhide Kid* were Jack Davis, Dick Ayers, Jack Keller and Paul Reinman. In 1964 Stan Lee's brother, Larry Lieber, took over both the scripting and the pencilling. In 1973 *Rawhide Kid* was transformed into a reprint comic book, with no original material any longer published.

One year after *Rawhide Kid*, Atlas followed with *Matt Slade, Gunslinger,* another of Stan Lee's Western confections. Matt Slade was one more incarnation of that durable Western staple, the lone rider of the plains. After he had outwitted, outfought, outridden and outgunned any number of opponents, he would be asked to stay on the ranch by some beseeching and panting young maiden he had just rescued, to whose entreaties he would invariably answer: "I'd like to stay, ma'am, but ... I'm too restless to stay in one place very long!" *Matt Slade* never caught on despite some good artwork by Williamson and Torres (and a change of title to *Kid Slade*), and it was one of those to disappear in 1957.

One 1956 comic book of somewhat longer duration was put out by those inexhaustible purveyors of Western fare, Charlton Comics. Called *Texas Rangers in Action*, it claimed the stories were drawn from real cases out of the files of the famous corps of lawmen after the fashion of King Vidor's 1937 movie, *The Texas Rangers*. Each story would usually start out with a written introduction to get quickly past the dull preliminaries and smack into the middle of the action. Thus a story titled "Badland Friend" would open with the following words: "This was the Texas badlands ... where comancheros traded fire-arms to the renegades and owl-hooters ... where everyman's hand was against the lawman! It was here that Texas Ranger Rudd Ferril caught up with the men who had looted the Centralia Bank . . ," while the first picture would show the afore-mentioned Ferril shooting it out with the robbers.

Another story, "Bart Frisco," was told entirely in the second person. "You are Bart Frisco, an ornery shrimp, born with a grudge against the whole normal-sized world and dead bent on living off another man's sweat," the invisible narrator would intone, and Bart Frisco would be depicted playing havoc in ranch and saloon before getting his come-uppance at the hands of some steely-eyed Ranger.

Despite mediocre artwork and laborious writing, the book's emphasis on slam-bang action and fast-moving plot payed off. *Texas Rangers* was fairly successful and survived the lean years of the Sixties, adding a continuing feature, *The Man Called Loco*, to their tired formula around the middle of the decade. The book was finally discontinued in August 1970.

In 1956 the Winchester-Western Division of Olin Mathieson Chemical Corporation (now simply the Olin Corporation) put out a one-shot giveaway comic book called *The Gun That Won the West*, with the subtitle "The Story of Winchester." Giveaway comic books were nothing new of course. As a matter of fact, the first genuine comic book ever produced in the United States, *Funnies on Parade*, had been distributed by the Procter and Gamble Company in 1933 as a promotion gimmick for their products. The role played by

-- BUT OLIVER WINCHESTER, A SUCCESSFUL MERCHANT AND MANUFACTURER, BROUGHT IMPROVED PRODUCTION METHODS AND IMAGINATIVE SALES TECHNIQUES TO THE ARMS INDUSTRY.

THESE QUALITIES, PLUS WINCHESTER'S FAITH IN THE FUTURE AND HIS WILLINGNESS TO PERSONALLY ADVANCE FUNDS TO HIS COMPANY, PLAYED A LARGE PART IN THE EVENTUALLY SUCCESSFUL SEARCH FOR A SOUND REPEATING RIFLE.

AS FOR MILITARY WEAPONS, AS EARLY AS 1903, T.C. JOHNSON WAS DEVELOPING FOR WINCHESTER A LINE OF SEMI-AUTOMATIC OR SELF-LOADING RIFLES, UTILIZING THE GAS PRESSURE IN THE BREECH TO BLOW BACK THE MECHANISM AND AUTOMATICALLY RELOAD.

IT WAS THIS PRINCIPLE WHICH LED TO THE DEVELOPMENT OF THE M1 CARBINE, SO HIGHLY REGARDED FOR ITS EASE OF OPERATION, RUGGEDNESS, AND LIGHT WEIGHT, BY G.I.'S OF WORLD WAR II. WINCHESTER DESIGNED AND PRODUCED FOR THE GOVERNMENT NEARLY A MILLION OF THEM.

Jack King, *The Gun That Won the West*. This comic book established a legitimate tie-in between the West and one of its legends, the Winchester rifle. © Olin Corporation.

such real and fictional Western figures as the Lone Ranger, Tom Mix and Hopalong Cassidy in the promotion of breakfast cereals and sundry products has already been well documented in these pages; let us also mention Red Ryder and Little Beaver hawking B.B. guns on the back covers of their comic books.

In all those cases the relationship between the medium and the message had been purely arbitrary, and in some cases far-fetched; the Olin Mathieson comic book, however, was different and worthy of special notice, in that it established a legitimate tie-in between the West and one of its long-lasting legends, that of the Winchester rifle.

Under a dramatic wrap-around cover painted by artist Paul Laune, and depicting in vivid fashion a wagon train slowly winding its way across the western plains, the comic book managed to present a wealth of informative features within its 24 pages. There was a two-page photographic report on the making of the Winchester rifle, a centerfold spread depicting the models currently available, five pages of tips on how to become a good rifleman, and some more guidelines for the benefit of hunters!

The most interesting part of the pamphlet, however, was the first eight pages, which illustrated in a forthright and pleasant manner the role played by firearms (and more specifically by Winchester guns) in the opening and taming of the West. "All through the pages of American history, firearms have been a dramatic and indispensable tool to those pioneers who push forward the frontiers of civilization," the story opened, and then went on to record the invention of the repeating rifle by B. Tyler Henry, under the enlightened guidance of Oliver F. Winchester.

From there the narrator lightly touched on real incidents in which the Winchester rifle played an important part, from the Indian wars to the Juarez rebellion in Mexico to Theodore Roosevelt's charge up San Juan Hill. There is one incident worth recording here: "Marshal Steve Venard of Nevada City once set out alone after three bandits. As he trailed them, one of the bandits leaped from concealment . . . but before he could pull his trigger, Venard had dropped him! A swift flip of the lever action, and before the echoes of the first shot had died away Venard had killed the second bandit, and turned his attention to the third! He missed one shot . . . but scored with the fourth and the posse arrived to find three dead thieves. The whole affair had taken a matter of seconds . . ."

Some odd bits of knowledge can be gleaned from the lively narrative ably illustrated by Jack King: that Annie Oakley and Antarctic explorer Sir Ernest Shackleton were both admirers of the Winchester rifle, for instance; or that Buffalo Bill himself once wrote to the Winchester Company, telling how one of its rifles had saved his life when a wounded bear had charged after him.

In 1957 the little-known Farrell Publications issued two short-lived Western comic books, *Apache Trail* and *The Rider*. The former dealt mainly with purported incidents from the Apache wars, while the latter featured another in the endless horde of masked avengers, this one operating in Arizona and New Mexico. For a rugged Western hero the Rider had some strange mannerisms, including the quaint exclamation, "Leaping Gila monsters!" which he used on almost every occasion. The two Farrell publications had the further distinction of sporting some of the best looking covers and some of the most execrable interior art ever to be found in any comic book.

In the mid-Fifties Warner Brothers introduced the popular *Maverick* TV series, and Dell followed suit in 1958 by issuing a *Maverick* comic book. The first issue had a photograph of James Garner in his role as Bret Maverick with a deck of cards in his hands, while a blurb proudly proclaimed: "Trouble was his trade . . . and he knew all the answers."

Bret Maverick was an inveterate gambler who roamed the West of the post-Civil War days, forever on a sharp lookout for a friendly poker game and a fast buck. His foil and companion was his brother Bart (played on TV by Jack Kelly). The comic book usually followed the basic plot of the series: Bret or Bart getting reluctantly talked into helping an old man and his young and, of course, sexy daughter out of some trouble or other. The Maverick brothers would generally win the day, more by their wits than by their guns.

The stories were pretty straightforward and departed from the TV screenplays in many ways. For instance they did not feature *Maverick*'s free-floating cast of characters, such as Samantha Crawford, Gentleman Jim Dandy, Pappy Maverick, or cousin Beau. On the other hand they made copious use of the famous $1,000 dollar bill the Maverick brothers reverently pinned to the inside of one of their jackets, as bait for unscrupulous operators.

The best thing in the Dell version was Dan Spiegle's art job. The Western was Spiegle's forte as his work on the *Hopalong Cassidy* newspaper strip amply dem-

Dan Spiegle, *Maverick*. This comic book adaptation of the popular TV Western series was the work of Dan Spiegle, one of the most prolific illustrators of the Western scene. © Dell Publishing Company.

onstrated, and with *Maverick* he gave a good account of himself. Moving his pen like a camera, Spiegle told the story functionally and pleasantly, carrying the book until its demise in 1962.

The decade of the Fifties went out with a bang (fired no doubt from a six-shooter). From 1955 to 1959 cowboys, Indians, lawmen and outlaws of every stripe and description pursued their unending parade. There was *The Kid From Texas* and *The Kid From Dodge City*, and *The Kid From Montana*, later changed to *Montana Kid*. One Atlas comic book called *Billy Buckskin* became *Two-Gun Western*; then, in an effort to top itself, the same publisher put out *Six-Gun Western* perhaps in the hope it would sell three times as fast as the former title. Among a long roster of evocative titles let us briefly mention *Sheriff of Tombstone*, *Quick-Trigger Western* (graced with artwork from Gray Morrow, Bill Everett, Reed Crandall, and others), *Western Trails*, *Blazing Sixguns*, and *Wild Western Roundup*.

From the Sixties to the Seventies

After the heady decade of the Fifties the next 15 years were a period of retrenchment, even of blight, for the Western comic book. Stan Lee's regeneration of the super-hero format dealt a heavy blow to the more down-to-earth Western hero; many titles were discontinued in the Sixties and Seventies, with precious few creations coming out to take their place.

From 1960 through 1967 one would be hard-pressed to find any new Western title worthy of interest, let alone original or innovative. Dell's *Idaho* (1963-65), Super-Comics' *Gunfighters* (1963-64), and Charlton's *The Gunfighters*, all lasted for only a few issues, and are better left forgotten.

Montana Kid. © Charlton Comics.

Mighty Marvel Western. This is the cover of one of the current Western comic books. © Marvel Comics Group.

The first Western comic book to take a leaf from Stan Lee's "super-heroes with problems" was *Bat Lash*. Bat Lash was a friendly, easygoing plainsman who, under his smiling exterior, hid a troubled past, and a disturbed, even neurotic, mind. He was a lone wolf, without emotional ties, and despite all the young girls who threw themselves at him, without love. As written by Sergio Aragones and drawn by Nick Cardy, Bat Lash's adventures came closer to the world of hard-boiled detective fiction than to the tradition of the West. The stories relied on mood and characterization rather than on slam-bang action. The comic book's intentions were commendable but they failed to register with the readers. Started in 1968, *Bat Lash* was dropped the next year.

In 1968 Marvel consolidated a number of their Western features into one umbrella title, *Mighty Marvel Western*. The first 20 issues were devoted to reprints of *Kid Colt*, *Rawhide Kid* and *Two-Gun Kid*, with *Matt Slade/Kid Slade* and *The Ringo Kid* added later on. The comic book gave a new generation of young readers a chance to get acquainted with some of the best stories of the Western's golden age. It also gave older readers an opportunity to catch up on those tales they may have missed earlier, since the editors were thoughtful enough to indicate the origin of each reprinted story.

The format proved so successful that not only is *Mighty Marvel Western* still going strong, but it also incited Marvel's main competitor, National Periodicals, to follow the leader as they have so often done in the past. In 1970 National resuscitated their old title, *All Star Western*, for the purpose.

At first the *All Star* comic books were, like the rival *Mighty Marvel*, chiefly filled with reprint material; however, because National had a smaller backlist of Western stories than Marvel, original material began to creep in. There was a weak version of *Billy the Kid*, and *El Diablo*, a goodish tale of a Zorro-type masked rider, by Gary Morrow. But the star of the series was to make his entrance only in issue No. 10: it was *Jonah Hex*.

Jonah Hex was an embittered ex-officer of the Confederacy who had had the right side of his face blown away by gunfire on the last days of the Civil War. Since then he had been roaming the West, torn between good and evil, each personified by a different side of his face. It is worth noting at this juncture that the Jekyll-and-Hyde theme of the disfigured outsider had been explored previously in comics, notably in *Batman* with Two-Face, but he was an out-and-out villain, while Jonah Hex is pretty much the hero, albeit of a reluctant sort.

Michael Fleischer and George (Jorge) Moliterni, *Jonah Hex*. Jonah Hex is a Western variation on the Jekyll-and-Hyde theme of dual personality. © DC Comics, Inc.

Hex can sometimes be callous but never intentionally evil. At one point he allowed a woman to be hanged despite the entreaties of his sidekick, Redeye Charlie. His wrath will always turn against those clever crooks, high-placed manipulators and corrupt lawmen that are forever crossing paths with the disfigured rider. Hex's nemesis is the Yellow Mask gang against which he wages an unrelenting and deadly guerilla war.

The artwork of *Jonah Hex* has been entrusted to a stable of talented foreign artists: first the Filipinos Tony de Zuñiga and Noly Panaligan, later followed by the Latin Americans George (Jorge) Moliterni and José-Luis García López. The theme and the illustrators have proved extremely successful, so much so that *Jonah Hex* has now practically taken over the contents of *Weird Western Tales* as the book is now called, starting with issue No. 11, and it has become the most popular Western feature among comic books of the Seventies.

Also of note is the attempted revival of *The Outlaw Kid* by Marvel in 1970. Made up almost exclusively of reprints in its first issues, it later added original material. Only second-rate artists and writers were as-

Stan Lee and Syd Shores, *Red Wolf*. Red Wolf was the adaptation of the costumed super-hero to the Western genre. © Marvel Comics Group.

signed to the new features, however, and the *Outlaw Kid* expired for the second time in March 1975.

A boomlet seemed to be developing at the beginning of the Seventies; in 1971 the newly-formed Skywald Comics brought out *Butch Cassidy* in the wake of the successful Paul Newman-Robert Redford movie. There had been at least one other comic book devoted to the notorious outlaw, Avon's 1951 *Butch Cassidy and the Wild Bunch*. Skywald, however, was a company being run on a shoe-string and *Butch Cassidy* did not come up to much anyway, and the comic book sank along with its publishers later that year.

In 1972 Marvel tried one more stab at the Western genre with *Red Wolf*, which was to be one of the last Western titles of any consequence put out by a comic book publisher to date. Subtitled "Indian Avenger of the Western Plains," *Red Wolf* had a run of only nine issues, ending its career in September 1973; yet short as its existence was, *Red Wolf* was original enough to be remembered with respect.

Red Wolf was Stan Lee's and Gardner Fox's adaptation of the costumed super-hero to the Western genre. Army scout Johnny Wakely, working out of Fort Rango under Colonel Sabre, was in actuality the last descendant in a long line of Cheyenne justice-fighters, the *Owayodata*. Wearing the wolf headdress, the *Owayo Ata'hae*, and armed only with his quarterstaff,

Red Wolf fulfilled his mission to be brother to and protector of all men, be they red or white. His foes have included not only the garden-variety of evil-doers, such as horse thieves, gun runners and cattle rustlers, but also more esoteric malefactors, as, for instance, a horned horseman called Koumt'ou Kia, the demon rider of the plains. Red Wolf was human, too, and he would sometimes dream of casting off his wolf-head and joining the pretty and tender Fawn, patiently waiting for him. But that was never to be, because: "The spirit voice of the *Owayodata* summons . . . and the wolfhead warrior must obey!"

Gary Friedrich and Syd Shores, *The Gunhawks*. This attempt at an "integrated" Western unfortunately did not last long. © Marvel Comics Group.

The theme of the mysterious avenger is, of course, as old as comics themselves, but *Red Wolf* marked the first time that an American Indian had assumed the role, and it certainly should be remembered at least for breaking ground in a new direction, even if it proved temporarily unsuccessful.

As back-up features to *Red Wolf* there were *Lobo,* more specifically devoted to the wolfhead warrior's lupine companion, and a series of short pieces depicting in comic form the careers of famous and infamous figures from the historical West.

In October 1972, only a few months after *Red Wolf,* Marvel launched another ground-breaking Western title, *The Gunhawks.* The introductory title of the first story touted the new venture as "an all-new look at the wild, wild West," and it certainly was different. Reno Jones, a black cowboy, and Kid Cassidy, his fair-haired companion, were the title heroes—a pair of war buddies who had fought on the Confederate side in the War Between the States. To one old-timer expressing wonderment that he could have been a Reb, Reno Jones told how he witnessed the abduction of Rachel, his fiancée, by an unruly mob of Union soldiers, adding: "So I joined the Confederate Army . . . blinded from the causes of the war by the hatred which boiled in my blood! And I swore I'd kill every blue-uniformed soldier alive . . . or die trying . . ."

When the war was over, Reno Jones's tale continued, he and his childhood companion, Kid Cassidy, who was also the son of Jones's former plantation owner, joined forces in search of Rachel. During their quest they picked up a variety of clues, and were confronted by a number of enemies, such as stagecoach robbers, buffalo hunters, and Reb-hating Union veterans. Their first adventure, during which they met a half-crazed old prairie bum who had appointed himself the protector of the last herd of buffaloes in the region, was also one of their most entertaining.

In spite of fast plotting by Gary Friedrich and some excellent Syd Shores artwork, especially on the action scenes, *The Gunhawks* failed to catch fire. In issue No. 6 Kid Cassidy was killed off, and the feature then became the first black-hero Western in comics—a position deliberately taken in order to bolster sagging sales. The switch did not help, however, and *The Gunhawks* ended its career with issue No. 7 (October 1973).

No survey of the West in comic books would be complete without a salute to Dell's stolid and durable Four-Color Comics. Started under this title in 1941 the series had reached issue No. 1354 by the time of its discontinuance in 1962. Incidentally it should be noted that only the first 99 issues carried the logo "Four-Color" on the cover. During its 20-plus years of existence Four-Color performed yeoman service in the cause of Western comics. Its publishers reprinted a number of Western newspaper strips (*The Lone Ranger, King of the Royal Mounted, The Cisco Kid,* even *Red Ryder*) and served as testing grounds for

KNIGHTS OF THE RANGE

HEIRESS TO THE GREAT **RIPPLE RANCH**, YOUNG HOLLY RIPPLE, FACES A RANGE WAR TO HOLD HER VAST CATTLE HERDS! STEADYING HER IS OLD "CAPPY" BRITT.

AND SUPPORTING HOLLY WITH THEIR WILD, RECKLESS LOYALTY ARE A CREW OF HARDBITTEN YOUNG GUNFIGHTERS, HER "KNIGHTS OF THE RANGE," LED BY THE ERSTWHILE OUTLAW, RENN FRAYNE.

Zane Grey, *Knights of the Range*. Zane Grey's novels and stories were almost all transposed to the comic book medium. © Dell Publishing Company.

later comic book titles (*Gene Autry* and *Roy Rogers* started there, for instance). They also adapted in comic book form the novels of Zane Grey (*West of the Pecos, Riders of the Purple Sage, Fighting Caravans, Wilderness Trek*, among others) and Luke Short (*Six Gun Ranch, King Colt, Bounty Guns*, etc.), thus keeping them alive for a new generation of readers.

Nor did Four-Color's editors turn uniquely to the printed page for inspiration; their cross-media comprehensiveness extended to movies and television as well. They regularly presented their readers with such film adaptations as *The Left-Handed Gun, The Indian Fighter*, Howard Hawks's *Rio Bravo*, and John Ford's *The Searchers* and *The Horse Soldiers*, while TV's *Bat Masterson, Have Gun Will Travel, Bonanza, Gunsmoke* and *Tales of Wells Fargo* all found a spot in Four-Color's hospitable pages.

The West is currently out of fashion in comic books. There are only a handful of surviving comic titles, a far cry from the halcyon days of the Fifties. Yet, as the pendulum seems once again to swing away from the super-heroes, the cowboys are bound to make a comeback at a triumphant gallop, bringing with them a refreshing whiff of clean, open-space fun into a medium that has grown increasingly stale and claustrophobic.

CHAPTER THREE

THE WEST IN THE COMICS

© Walt Disney Productions

While the treatment of the West, its tradition and representation, are only peripheral to the non-Western comic strips, no image of the West in the comics would be complete without some recognition of the ubiquitousness and universality of the Western theme.

As we have seen in chapter one, the American West appeared in the comics well before the Western strip, as a distinct genre, had been established. The oldest comic strip in existence, *The Katzenjammer Kids*, did not fail in this respect, even after it had passed from the hands of Rudolph Dirks to those of Harold Knerr. There was a very funny 1915 sequence in which the Kids, traveling with their entourage through the country by private railroad car, finally settled on the ranch of Der Captain's old friend, Cayuse Pete, where they promptly wreaked havoc on their parents, the ranch hands, the cook Ching-a-Ling, and the neighboring Indians.

Not to be outdone, Dirks himself catapulted Hans and Fritz to the West in the Twenties in his strip retitled *The Captain and the Kids* (he had lost the rights to the Katzenjammer name, following a 1913 court decision), where the Kids showed themselves hardly less destructive than they had been in Knerr's version a few years earlier.

Go west, young man (and woman too)

Hairbreadth Harry by the prolific C.W. Kahles, which many regard as the first adventure strip worthy of the name, opened in fact on a Western scene, when our boy-hero, as he was then described, through fast thinking and even faster riding, was able, by bringing in the governor's pardon, to save the life of an innocent prospector unjustly sentenced to death. From then on Harry was to show himself as a frequent visitor to the wide Western spaces along with his sweetheart Belinda Blinks, and with the top-hatted Rudolph Rassendale in hot pursuit. One such adventure in 1907, for instance, involved a gold mine, claim jumping, ambush and skulduggery, as well as several gunfights and a final landslide that saved the hero and Belinda—in the nick of time, naturally—from the clutches of their pursuers.

Harry's chief competition, Harry Hershfield's *Desperate Desmond*, had at least one sequence (in 1910) set in the West, where the hero, Claude Eclair, and his beloved Rosamund had settled on a ranch. The couple's arch-enemy, Desperate Desmond, top-hatted and black-coated, as befits a stage villain, tried to do Claude in on a multitude of occasions, dropping him into a well or sicking a wild bull on him, all to no avail. If anything the humor in *Desmond* was even more outrageous than in Kahles's strip, and the Western scenery served only as a backdrop to the shenanigans. It was a pretty wild and woolly backdrop at that, but it helped familiarize comic strip readers with what would later become a cliché, that of the West's open spaces and limitless opportunities.

Harold Knerr, *The Katzenjammer Kids*. Soon after taking over the "Katzies" in 1914, Knerr catapulted the two infernal twins into a rollicking Far West adventure. © King Features Syndicate.

Rube Goldberg, *Boob McNutt.* Despite the best of intentions the well-named Boob always got into one zany predicament after another. © Rube Goldberg.

Sol Hess and Wallace Carlson, *The Nebbs.*
"Sheriff" Rudy Nebb in one of his legendary
exploits. © Bell Syndicate.

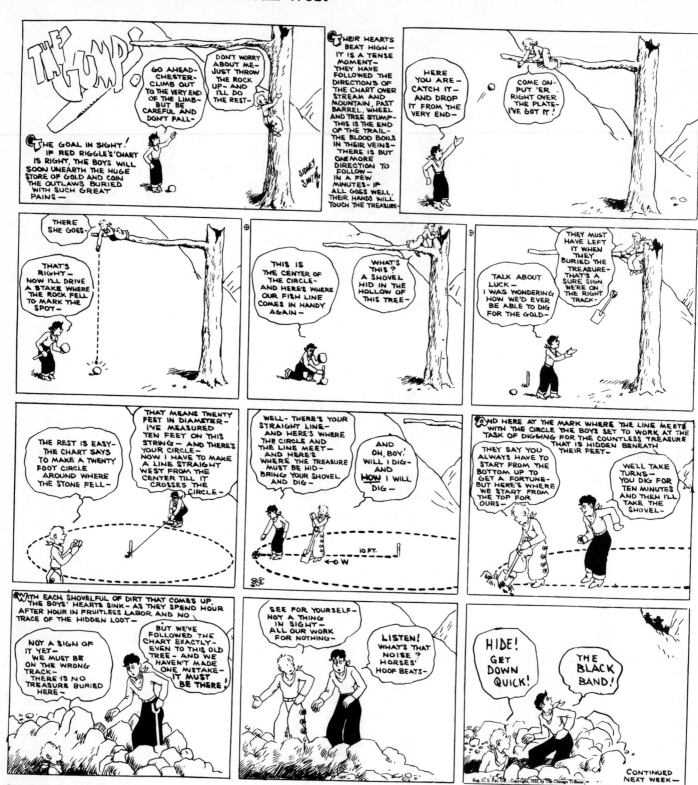

Sidney Smith, *The Gumps*. Chester Gump and his pal in a wild treasure hunt out West. © Chicago Tribune-New York News Syndicate.

Rube Goldberg, himself a native of California, utilized a Western motif on more than one occasion in the course of his comic strip career, one of the first being a zany *Boob McNutt* Sunday sequence of 1918, in which the sap-headed innocent found himself in a variety of predicaments (shot from a cliff, running from stampeding cattle, rolled after a pinochle game by a suave Mexican outlaw, etc.), all of this purportedly taking place in the wild country around Mad Dog Gulch.

Perhaps one of the funniest Western episodes occurred in the domestic strip, *The Nebbs*. In 1927 Rudy Nebb and his family went west on a vacation, and this gave author Sol Hess an opportunity to weave some wild adventures around Rudy's imaginary reminiscences of the time when he was sheriff of Wild Cat Gulch. The exploits of Sheriff Nebb, and his epic confrontations with Bad Eye Bodie, the local outlaw, were concocted with great relish and gusto by Hess, and the wild goings-on were skillfully depicted by artist Wallace Carlson in a mixture of "big foot" style and tongue-in-cheek realism.

Sol Hess had been the chief scriptwriter of *The Gumps* a decade before, and not to be outdone, Sidney Smith in 1933 had his juvenile hero Chester Gump, and his pal Jerry, dig up a cache of gold hidden by a gang of outlaws in the American Desert. There were thrills, chases, and dramatic twists a-plenty as the boys gamely set out on their task in a story that was a cross between Edgar Allan Poe's *The Gold Bug* and Robert Louis Stevenson's *Treasure Island*.

Even Maggie and Jiggs ventured west, along with their daughter Nora and their English son-in-law, in the course of a 1939 trip around the U.S.A. that is one of the funniest sequences of *Bringing Up Father*. This gave George McManus one more occasion to exercise his sharp wit at the expense of the city-slickers by showing the Indians and the assorted cow country types always one up on the visiting dudes. McManus must have had so much fun with the situation that he sent his bickering couple back for more in 1941.

As many astute observers have remarked, Harold Gray's social philosophy, as presented in his *Little Orphan Annie*, comes very close to the ethics of frontier America in its advocacy of strong-arm tactics and vigilante justice. Yet Gray did not get around to putting his waif into a Western setting before 1941. In the course of the sequence Annie, her billionaire protector Daddy Warbucks, his sinister bodyguard Punjab, and her dog Sandy all go west in order to investigate some trouble in one of Warbucks's mines. With the help of some hocus-pocus Punjab gets rid of one of the troublemakers, Hooting Owl, the medicine-man of a neighboring Indian tribe, and becomes honorary Indian chief under the name of Peeping Tom! After a number of alarums, double-crosses, and sundry excursions, Annie and her cohorts finally prevail, and calm is restored.

As usual Gray introduced into the narrative some colorful characters, like Forty-Four John, the grizzled gold prospector; and the chief of the saboteurs, the oily and menacing Scuttle. Most picturesque of all, however, was the old Indian chief, whom Gray depicted as full of traditional wisdom as well as of well-worn aphorisms. "Time passes swiftly when one wrestles in the darkness with the black spirit," he would sententiously mutter to Forty-Four John just out of a coma. All in all this was one of *Annie's* most memorable adventures.

Harold Gray, *Little Orphan Annie.* ©
Chicago Tribune-New York News Syndicate.

Little Orphan Annie's main competitor in the waif business, Little Annie Rooney, had also her share of Western vicissitudes while fleeing with her dog Zero from the clutches of "heartless, cruel Mrs. Meany," her lawful and rapacious foster mother. Once, in the mid-Thirties, she found refuge with a gold-hearted (no pun intended) prospector in the Southwest desert, but Mrs. Meany's minions were hot on her trail, and she had to move away fast (to Hollywood, as it turned out).

A weirder sequence of the late Forties had Annie wandering into a lost oasis in the middle of "Dead Man's Desert," where she met a ten-century-old hermit living among a peace-loving tribe of Indians. This Western Shangri-la was soon overrun by would-be

Brandon Walsh and Nicholas Afonsky, *Little Annie Rooney*. Like her companion in misfortune, Little Orphan Annie, Little Annie Rooney was no stranger to the West. © King Features Syndicate.

kidnapers, bounty hunters and maddened Indians, and Annie had to flee again. Brandon Walsh, who wrote *Little Annie Rooney*, was not as adept at characterization as Harold Gray, but his long-bearded and somnambulistic hermit was possibly one of the weirdest characters to come out of the comic strip.

Lost Indian tribes have always seemed to exercise a strange fascination over comic strip artists of every genre. The talented Frank Godwin was no exception. In the mid-Thirties, in his strip *Eagle Scout Roy Powers*, he took the titular hero and his sidekick Chunky to the American Desert, where they promptly stumbled upon a tribe which had miraculously escaped the white man's notice. At first the Indians wanted to keep the two scouts as their permanent prisoners but, after Roy had saved the chief's daughter, they were released upon their word of honor not to reveal the red men's abode.

In the early Fifties Godwin returned to the theme in *Rusty Riley* (the continuity being written by his brother Harold). This time Rusty and his girl companion Patty Miles discovered a race of midget horses in the recesses of the Grand Canyon. In both adventures Godwin displayed his love of the outdoors and his knowledge of the West and of Indian lore in his truthfully rendered drawings of landscapes, buildings and costumes.

Ed Wheelan, *Minute Movies*. In his delightful spoof of silent movies, Wheelan often chose a Western locale, as in this example. © George Matthew Adams Service.

Ed Wheelan, *Minute Movies.*
© George Matthew Adams
Service.

The most constant exponent of the Western motif in comic strips, from the late Teens on, was Edgar Wheelan, first in his *Midget Movies*, and later with his even more popular *Minute Movies*. In his continuities Wheelan would often good-naturedly kid the William S. Hart and Tom Mix horse-operas of the period. One of these satires, "The Mysterious Bandit," was trailered thus: "On this screen starting tomorrow will be shown the greatest Western picture ever filmed. In fact a super-serial de luxe with all the Wheelan movie stars . . ."; and the author went on to proclaim (tongue in cheek): "No lover of the golden West can afford to miss this sensational five-part serial, full of the romance and glamor of the old mining days!"

The plots, while full of self-mocking fun, were also suspenseful: Wheelan knew how to end each daily episode with a cliff-hanger worthy of *The Perils of Pauline:* heroine tied down to a railroad track, or carried away screaming by a sneering outlaw; hero locked up in a flaming cabin, or facing a roomful of rattlesnakes, and every other piece of such enjoyable nonsense.

George Herriman, *Krazy Kat.* Krazy, in a typical pose, plucking the guitar and singing a ditty made famous by Pancho Villa's raiders. © King Features Syndicate.

George Herriman's *Krazy Kat* does not immediately come to mind when discussing the myth of the West in American comic strips; yet the author deliberately chose a recognizable Western locale as the backdrop to the interplay between the eternal triangle formed by Krazy, Ignatz and Offissa Pupp. Even when the mood is most tender and lyrical, the author never stops winking at us, like having Krazy plucking the guitar and singing *Valentina, Valentina* ("Una Pasión Me Domina"), a ditty made famous on either side of

Roy Crane, *Captain Easy.* Soldier-of-fortune Easy and his pint-sized companion, Wash Tubbs, dressed up in full Western regalia.
© NEA Service.

the border by Pancho Villa's raiders; and the hanging moon, shifting rock formations, and dancing saguaro cacti of Coconino County's "enchanted mesa" are the figments of Herriman's (and Everyman's) dream of the American West.

Big country, big men

The American West has always held a strong fascination for the many adventurers plying the comic pages in the Thirties and for their creators who knew that when everything else fails you can always fall back on a Western. No comic strip hero was deemed complete until he had had least one encounter with the big and wild country beyond the Missouri.

Roy Crane's pint-sized hero, Wash Tubbs, and his square-jawed companion, the adventuring Captain Easy, for instance, chased their sworn enemy, Bull Dawson, through the Nevada Desert, went ranching on a Montana cattle spread, and put many an outlaw out

Lee Falk and Phil Davis, *Mandrake*. The
magician's playing some tricks on the
natives. © King Features Syndicate.

to pasture, in the unending cascade of fast-paced incidents that form the lively canvas of *Captain Easy*.

A frequent visitor to the West was Mandrake the Magician, who came out to the range in his usual white-tie-and-tails outfit, to the thigh-slapping merriment of the local citizenry; a merriment that turned to awe, however, when Mandrake unleashed his astounding hypnotic powers. In a 1938 Sunday adventure, for instance, Mandrake and his herculean black assistant Lothar went to investigate the mysterious goings-on on a New Mexico ranch haunted by a two-headed monster. Of course this was only an underhanded trick to force the owner of the ranch, a comely brunette named Donna, to sign over her property to a gang of crooks. In the course of this episode, Mandrake pitted his magic against the taunts of his rival, Harker, the ranch foreman who at one point advised him: "You better change these duds, greenhorn. They won't last long out here!" When Harker managed to stay on a bucking broncho for four minutes, Mandrake simply sat on the animal, miraculously suspended in mid-air, for half an hour. After Harker had dropped a bull in three minutes, Mandrake with a simple wave of the hand, turned the bull upside down in a split second!

Another entertaining adventure occurred in 1949-50, when Mandrake again had to prove his mettle by beating the jeering cowpunchers at their own game. After watching the sharpest shooting cowboy plug a hole in a silver dollar with one bullet, Mandrake did him one better, hitting the coin which was instantly transformed into the exact change! A more dangerous game was afoot, however, with a ruthless band of

William Ritt and Clarence Gray, *Brick Bradford*. In this Sunday Western episode Gray displays his striking powers of depiction and his incomparable artistry. © King Features Syndicate.

outlaws attacking trains in the region and robbing passengers. The top-hatted magician would put an end to their depredations with such tricks as making a locomotive fly into the air in front of the terror-stricken bandits.

There are a dozen or more Mandrake adventures which have practically plumbed all the major themes of the modern Western: land manipulation, political chicanery, terror campaign, bank robbery, etc. Lee Falk, the creator of *Mandrake*, has a lively feeling for the West, and this interest is reflected in his entertaining scripts.

Brick Bradford was another newspaper strip which often utilized Western plots and backgrounds. William Ritt, the scriptwriter, and Clarence Gray, the artist, were both fond of the wide open spaces and knowledgeable in Indian lore and legend. They would go back to the Western again and again, as to a fountain of youth, all through the Thirties, Forties and Fifties.

Brick's longest Western adventure took place in 1940, in the episode titled "The Diamond Doll." Charged by Professor Van Atta Salisbury to recover an ancient Indian doll (nicknamed the "Diamond Doll" because of its jewel eyes) which had been stolen by a gang of thugs while on display at the Museum of Natural History in New York, Brick, his sidekick Bucko O'Brien, and the professor's daughter June, traveled to the place in the Southwest where the doll had originally come from. In the course of his investigations Brick was to discover that the doll was the key to a buried treasure; after a protracted struggle against the thieves who were also on the lookout for the treasure, he located the cache, but an explosion set up by the gangsters buried it forever (an ironic twist that Ritt was to use more than once, well before filmmaker John Huston made it into his trademark in similar circumstances).

The Gun That Won the West. © Olin Corporation

THE STORY OF WINCHESTER
THE GUN THAT WON THE WEST

24 Pages of Exciting
ADVENTURE
HUNTING AND
SHOOTING TIPS
and how to join the
Winchester Rifle Patrol

BUFFALO BILL, THAT MIGHTY PLAINSMAN, ONCE WROTE
TO THE WINCHESTER COMPANY, TELLING HOW ONE
OF ITS RIFLES SAVED HIS LIFE WHEN A WOUNDED
BEAR CHARGED HIM FROM THIRTY FEET AWAY. "...BEFORE
HE COULD REACH ME," WROTE BILL, "I HAD ELEVEN
BULLETS IN HIM, WHICH WAS A LITTLE MORE THAN
HE COULD COMFORTABLY DIGEST."

LITTLE ANNIE OAKLEY, TOO, USED
WINCHESTER RIFLES. NEEDLESS TO SAY,
THE COMPANY WAS PROUD TO PUBLICIZE
THE FACT THAT ITS GUNS WERE CHOSEN
BY SUCH STAR PERFORMERS.

The Gun That Won the West. © Olin Corporation.

Fred Harman, *Red Ryder.* Harman poured into *Red Ryder* all the
experience and knowledge he had learned previously on *Bronc
Peeler,* and made the feature into the most popular and acclaimed
Western strip of all time. © NEA Service.

Jesús Blasco, *Los Guerilleros*. The noted Spanish cartoonist Jesús Blasco created *Los Guerilleros* in 1968. The graphic style is striking and the composition elaborate and eye-catching as in this example. © Jesús Blasco.

Al McKimson, *Roy Rogers*. In the Fifties it seemed that every Western movie star got his own comic strip. *Roy Rogers* was a typical product of the time. © King Features Syndicate.

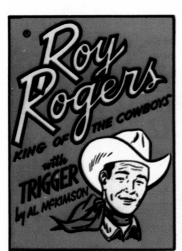

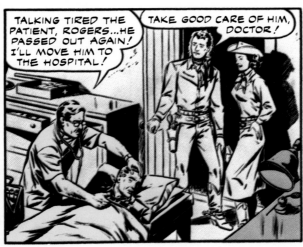

Allen Saunders and Elmer Woggon, *Chief Wahoo*. The strip was an early Western parody and a forerunner of such present-day satires as *Tumbleweeds* and *Redeye*. It later evolved into a straight adventure strip rechristened *Steve Roper*. © Field Newspaper Syndicate.

Jean-Michel Charlier and Jean Giraud, *Lieutenant Blueberry*. This strip is without doubt the most vigorous, exciting and refreshing Western since the early *Red Ryder*. It is also one of the most widely read and admired comic strips in France. © Editions Dargaud.

Ed Leffingwell, *Little Joe*. *Little Joe* is chiefly remembered for its often gripping narratives of the Thirties and Forties, and for Leffingwell's masterly depictions of Western scenes and situations. © Chicago Tribune-New York News Syndicate.

Fred Harman, *Bronc Peeler*. *Bronc Peeler* was Harman's first excursion into the world of Western comic strips. Although his graphic style was rough-hewn, his minutious depiction of horses, cattle and Western scenery made *Bronc Peeler* an appealingly authentic feature. © Fred Harman.

Stan Lee and Syd Shores, *Red Wolf*. *Red Wolf* was the adaptation of the costumed super-hero to the Western genre. It marked the first time that an American Indian had assumed the role and it broke new ground in comic books. © Marvel Comics Group.

Charles Flanders, *The Lone Ranger*. Born on the airwaves in 1933, *The Lone Ranger* rapidly became popular throughout the country. In 1938 the masked avenger received the double accolade of a movie serial and a newspaper strip devoted to his adventures. © King Features Syndicate.

Allen Dean and Zane Grey, *King of the Royal Mounted*. The scenery was one of the great assets of this excellent strip, from the frozen wastes of the Yukon to the vast expanses of the Canadian Prairies. One of the several illustrators of *King*, Allen Dean was by far the most talented. © King Features Syndicate.

Giovanni Bonelli and Aurelio Galleppini, *Tex Willer*. Created in 1948, *Tex Willer* is a highly entertaining Western strip that sometimes oversteps the boundaries of the genre. It has been a success from the start, and is probably the most popular comic strip in Italy today. © Edizioni Araldo.

CDC

COWBOY LOVE

A CHARLTON PUBLICATION

Cowboy Love

Nº 29

10¢

APPROVED BY THE COMICS CODE AUTHORITY

IN THIS ISSUE... OUTLAW GIRL·
·ROMANCE RENEGADE·

GALINDO & OSRIN

In this sequence the grandiose landscapes and endless vistas of the West were depicted with rare lyricism by Clarence Gray, one of the comics' most remarkable draftsmen.

Another of Brick's notable excursions into the world of the cowboys came in a 1951 sequence titled "Death Rock." The rock owed its name to the fact that a number of hardy souls had been killed trying to climb the lonely and funnel-like crag. While on vacation on a neighboring ranch Brick decided to fly in the face of superstition and of several death-threatening letters and to climb the rock. After getting to the summit Brick uncovered the rock's secret: a gold lode that unscrupulous operators had been mining clandestinely.

In this episode Gray again displays a rare mastery of evocation and suspense. The rock itself, forbiding in its lonely splendor, towers over the action, just as the majesty of the Western landscape towers over the pitiful doings of the humans below.

Even in the Sunday pages, where Brick's adventures were mostly devoted to science-fiction, Ritt and Gray could not help smuggling in some typically Western incidents. In 1937 Brick and yet another professor, Horatio Southern, left for a long journey into the future aboard the "time top." William Ritt took the opportunity to lovingly detail an Amerindian civilization of the year 6937 that had gone back to its origins. Caught by the aroused Indians while witnessing one of their secret ceremonies, Brick was sentenced to a series of ritual ordeals from which he, of course, emerged victorious.

The West has known quite a number of unlikely visitors in the comic pages, including some big-city detectives who, against all odds, felt as much at ease amid the wide open spaces as in the teeming streets of Chicago or Manhattan.

Secret agent X-9, for one, was no stranger to the

Cowboy Love. This cover symbolizes the popularity of the Western theme in comic books of the early Fifties. Cowboys were everywhere present—even in romance comics. © Charlton Comics.

West. Under the pen of Alex Raymond, he went there at least twice in cases both involving kidnaping. In the first episode, written by Dashiell Hammett in 1934, the G-man followed the kidnapers all the way to their hideout in Wyoming; the second sequence, written the following year, was even more Western-flavored with a full shoot-out involving the Texas Rangers who had come to X-9's rescue. In both adventures Raymond handled the Western scene with his customary assurance and elegance of line.

After *Secret Agent X-9* had passed to Charles Flanders, at least one 1937 sequence taking place in Oklahoma gave the new artist the opportunity to show that he could draw horses, wagons, Indians, and other essentials of the Western genre (a skill that Flanders had, of course, developed on *King of the Royal Mounted*). This was quite an entertaining episode that involved a wild scheme to pipe oil illegally, a series of attempts on X-9's life, and a threat to go on the warpath by a tribe of irate Indians in full regalia.

Dick Tracy is not a strip that most would associate with the West, but the eagle-nosed detective made several trips (some professional) to the big country. In 1940, for instance, he tracked down a fugitive from justice to the ranch where he was hiding out, after having posed as a rodeo rider—a fact made all the more outrageous by the criminal being a midget. This adventure was one of the most brutal of all the *Dick Tracy* sequences, and ended with a fight to the death between the detective (with one arm in a sling) and a 300-pound female bruiser, the midget's deadly associate.

The title of the most improbable Western of all, however, may belong to *Buck Rogers*. When the name

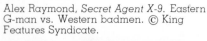

Alex Raymond, *Secret Agent X-9.* Eastern G-man vs. Western badmen. © King Features Syndicate.

Philip Nowlan and Dick Calkins, *Buck Rogers*. Or Western trails in the twenty-fifth century. © National Newspaper Syndicate.

Buck Rogers is recalled, images of rocket ships, flying belts and disintegrating pistols immediately spring to mind; yet Lieutenant Buck Rogers's first adventure in the America of the year 2429 is not so much a space-opera as it is a horse-opera.

After a brush with the Mongols occupying North America, Buck and his newfound girl companion Wilma Deering escape to the West which has largely returned to its untamed state, where they join the outlaws (in Western garb) who are fighting against Mongol rule. These include such colorful characters straight out of central casting as Two-Gun Pete, and a breezy fellow who announces himself and his intentions this way: "I'm th' Cyclone Kid from Dead Man's Gulch and I kin lick my weight in wild cats. Gimme thet gal!"

Buck has further to prove himself against Lariat Luke before being allowed to keep Wilma; he also becomes the boss of the outfit, and launches raiding parties on horseback against Mongol patrols. The odd mixture of the old and the new (the raiders were equipped with death rays and flying belts) probably did not work too well, for *Buck Rogers* authors Dick Calkins and Phil Nowlan soon gave it up. As it is, the entire sequence remains an interesting oddity.

Other adventure strips of note that have, at one time or other, utilized Western backgrounds for their protagonists, have included *Bobby Thatcher*, *Tailspin Tommy*, *Barney Baxter*, *Dickie Dare*, *The Adventures of Patsy*, and *Freckles and His Friends*, proving that the Western is a pervasive form that transcends the strict limits of the genre.

Here come the clowns!

The adventure strip artists have not been the only ones to latch on to Western adventure, as we have seen in the early part of this chapter. Later gag cartoonists from the late Twenties on have treated the theme not just for humoristic or satirical purposes, but in a vein that can only be called serio-comic. The most outstanding of these is probably E.C. Segar.

During the pre-Popeye days of *Thimble Theater*, Segar sent his two main characters, the irascible, shrimpish Castor Oyl, and his banana-nosed pal Ham Gravy, on a desert trek that lasted for two years, from 1928 to 1930, "one of the longest Sunday-page adventures in strip history," as comic strip historian Bill Blackbeard justly termed it. This was an incredible episode in which the two gold-seeking clowns found themselves confronted with brigands, buzzards and dust storms in an ever increasing crescendo.

Once Popeye had come onto the *Thimble Theater* stage things started really to perk up. The first Popeye

Western adventure came in 1933 when Popeye went to investigate mysterious shenanigans perpetrated by "the gold mine thieves" (this was also the title of the episode). The highlight of the sequence came when Popeye, disguised as a sultry saloon singer in order to get the goods on the miscreants, had to flatten every customer in the establishment after the affection-starved miners started throwing passes at the homely one-eyed sailor.

Bud Sagendorf, *Thimble Theater*. Popeye the Sailor in a typical display of super-human power. © King Features Syndicate.

Popeye's most celebrated Western adventure came in a 1935 Sunday sequence, with the irrepressible sailor, his sweetheart Olive, his adopted "infink" Swee'pea, and the intellectual moocher Wimpy on their way to Slither Creek to dig for gold. There were a wealth of hilarious, as well as finely observed, situations: Wimpy, after having traded away his food ration to hungry gold prospectors in exchange for gold, trying to wheedle Swee'pea's milk bottle away from the baby; or the same Wimpy, maddened with hunger, trying to mooch a hamburger from a candelabra cactus which his crazed mind imagines to be a lunch counter operator; then reciting a lyrical and death-obsessed poem of his own invention to a desert daisy before passing out.

Walt Disney, also, was a Western buff, as well as a member of Rancheros Visitadores, an association devoted to the preservation of the customs of Old California. A number of *Mickey Mouse* film cartoons had a Western background, a tradition that the later newspaper strip version, drawn and written by Floyd Gottfredson, enthusiastically followed.

Mickey's first full-fledged newspaper adventure (in 1930) involved the missing Uncle Mortimer, a map showing the location of a lost gold mine in Death Valley, and Mickey's two sworn enemies, Peg Leg Pete and Sylvester Shyster. After countless perils, predicaments and hilarious vicissitudes, Mickey and his girl friend Minnie finally reached Death Valley, found no gold, but discovered that their mysterious protector, "The Fox," was no other than Uncle Mortimer who had arranged the whole thing to unmask his crooked attorney!

Another Western adventure occurred in 1934, when Mickey and Minnie went on a vacation to Uncle Mortimer's ranch. Finding out that the local citizenry was being terrorized by a black-hooded villain called "the Bat Bandit," Mickey went to investigate only to find himself blamed for a series of bank robberies by the angry populace. Finally our hero was able to prove his innocence and to uncover the real thief, who turned out to be Don Jollio, Uncle Mortimer's trusted neighbor and the head of the local cattlemen's association.

Both these adventures ran in the dailies; but the West was just as prominently featured in the Sundays. In 1933 Mickey and his gang again traveled west to oversee Uncle Mortimer's ranch, while he was on a business trip to Australia. There was the usual quota of folderol going around involving cattle thieves, Minnie's abduction, and Mickey's ultimate victory.

In 1937 Mickey headed west again, in company this time of his bumbling companion, Goofy, in search of their fortune, to the lawless mining town of Nugget Gulch. Having earned the nicknames of "Little Poison" and "Big Poison," Mickey and Goofy were promptly made sheriff and deputy sheriff of the town, respectively. By luck and pluck they cleaned out the place, putting the notorious outlaw Pancho Malarky safely behind bars.

Mickey's companion and chief rival at the Disney studios, the cantankerous Donald Duck, has also had his share of Western adventures. One of the most memorable was depicted by the "duck artist" su-

Floyd Gottfredson, *Mickey Mouse.* The West was one of Mickey's favorite haunts. © Walt Disney Enterprises.

Carl Barks, *Donald Duck*. Dauntless deputy Donald Duck to the rescue. © Walt Disney Enterprises.

preme, Carl Barks, in a 1948 comic book story titled "Sheriff of Bullet Valley." While on a trip out west with his nephews, Huey, Louie, and Dewey, Donald, fired up by the screen exploits of his Western idols, Remington Rimfire, Carson Sage, Trigger Trueshot, Horace Mustang, and Sagebrush Savage, offered his services to help capture a gang of cattle rustlers that were decimating the herds of Bullet Valley. Overwhelmed by Donald's entreaties the local sheriff appointed the obnoxious duck as his deputy, sending him on his appointed rounds, ridiculously perched atop a huge palomino steed.

Outwitted at every turn by the gang leader, the snarling Blacksnake McQuirt, Donald was only saved thanks to the presence of mind of his nephews, who also engineered the capture of the whole band. Only Blacksnake escaped and fled, with Donald in hot pursuit, all through the Badlands. Although shot down by a hail of bullets and blasted by a hand grenade, Donald doggedly hung on, finally getting the drop on Blacksnake and putting him behind bars.

This story, one of the best ever done by Carl Barks, is now regarded as a classic of the genre. Barks was to return to the West in several more episodes ("In Old California," for instance), but none achieved the high degree of art, suspense, observation, and humor as "Sheriff of Bullet Valley."

The decline of Western newspaper strips has gone hand in hand with the general decline of adventure strips in recent times. The theme of the West is not quite dead yet, however; in 1968 *Secret Agent Corrigan*, as *Secret Agent X-9* is now called, had its G-man hero bottled up in a Western town, shooting it out with the crooked local sheriff and his henchmen. Frank O'Neal's *Short Ribs* features an inept sheriff, "still the slowest gun in the West," among its zany cast of characters. Then there is the "Lone Haranguer" who rouses the populace of Id in Johnny Hart's and Brant Parker's *The Wizard of Id*, with his defiant cry, "The King is a fink!" But these creations have unfortunately become increasingly scarce and far between. Only an improbable surge of interest in adventure strips among newspaper readers could bring back the West as a viable and exciting theme, as it was during the heyday of the Thirties.

Frank O'Neal, *Short Ribs*. A few of the weird denizens inhabiting O'Neal's legendary West. © NEA Service.

© Casa Ed. Universo

CHAPTER FOUR

WESTERNS AROUND THE WORLD

The epic of the West is a universal theme that transcends national frontiers and cultural traditions. From Europe to the Far East, and from the Pacific to South America, cartoonists have been mining this seemingly inexhaustible lode for a long time. There is a special fascination attaching to this portion of history (or legend) of the United States, a kind of visual dazzlement and symbolic imagery which make it particularly suitable to the comic strip medium.

The production of Western strips from foreign lands is immense and far outstrips (no pun intended!) the American contribution to the field, at least in numbers. It is not our purpose here to list each and every Western ever published around the globe, but to provide an overview of the genre, showing from a number of highlights how foreign artists have been able to translate and interpret the mythology of the American West.

BEAUCOUP DE GUERRIERS SONT DEMONTES, LES COW-BOYS VISANT LES CHEVAUX. DESEM-PARES PAR LA PERTE DE LEUR CHEF, DES PEAUX-ROUGES SE RENDENT.

LES DERNIERS CAVALIERS, VOYANT LE COUP MANQUE, S'ENFUIENT.

Le Rallic, *Teddy Bill*. French cartoonist Le Rallic was one of the most prolific purveyors of Western fare from the Thirties through the Fifties. © Editions du Lombard.

The French-speaking cowboys

In no other country has the American West been so consistently popular as in France. The very first French comic strip, Christophe's *La Famille Fenouillard*, a take-off on Jules Verne's *Around the World in Eighty Days*, had one of its episodes set in the West, where our hero was made a prisoner by a band of scalp-hunting Indians before being rescued by the U.S. Cavalry (1889). Many French comic strips were to follow this tradition: from *Les Pieds-Nickelés* to *Zig et Puce*, they had at least one obligatory sequence set in the wilds of America's West. One of the more hilarious of such episodes occurred in Hergé's famed *Tintin en Amérique* (1932), in which the lead character falls prey to countless vicissitudes after having accidentally discovered oil on an Indian reservation.

The Western became an established comic strip genre in France in the late Twenties—not far behind the United States. Le Rallic was probably its earliest practitioner. While his heroes all looked alike, with dour faces, red hair, and square jaws, the action was never monotonous. Gunfights, ambushes, stage-coach attacks, rodeos abounded. The story lines were shamelessly lifted from the movies, and one could find in Le Rallic's plots every cliché ever made familiar by William S. Hart and Broncho Bill Anderson. No matter, Le Rallic's feel for violent action was compelling, and his depiction of horses faultless, in innumerable strips such as *La Flèche du Soleil* ("The Arrow of the Sun"), *Jack Carter, Chevalier du Texas* ("Jack Carter, Texas Knight"), *Jojo Cowboy, Teddy Bill, Davy Crockett*, which he untiringly spun out all through the Thirties and Forties. Le Rallic's best-known creation is *Poncho Libertas*, a Western-type comic strip set in pre-war Mexico and centered around a daring band of rebels (1944-48). The theme may have been freedom-fighting, but the plot was pure horse-opera.

The scriptwriter of *Poncho Libertas* was Jacques Dumas, better known as Marijac, who had started his prolific career as a cartoonist. His first comic strip creation had been a Western, *Jim Boum*, which he was to draw, on and off, from 1934 to 1950. There was an endearing clumsiness to Marijac's draftsmanship (or lack of it) that was more than offset, however, by brilliant plotting and scripting. Marijac was a true Western buff (in the Forties he was made an honorary member of the Blackfoot tribe), and in *Jim Boum* he handled Western themes with both authenticity and affection.

Jim Boum himself was an archetypal Western hero, short on talk and long on action, in the tradition of the

Marijac (Jacques Dumas), *Jim Boum*. Marijac was a true Western buff who handled Western themes with both authenticity and affection. © Marijac.

times. He fought cattle rustlers, train robbers and outlaw gangs with the same aplomb and impassibility. These adventures were excitingly told and suspenseful, but Jim Boum was at his best when he was confronted with the uncaring elements, lost in the midst of a frightful blizzard, or caught in the swift currents of a treacherous river. There was more than a touch of pathos in Marijac's depiction of Jim's game and lonely figure valiantly braving the elemental powers of nature herself. Marijac was to draw a few more Westerns during his long and prolific career, such as *Joe Bing*, the parodic *Jim Clopin-Clopan*, but none proved equal to *Jim Boum*.

Morris (Maurice de Bevère), *Lucky Luke*. This tale of a "poor lonesome cowboy" is a funny and endearing take-off on all the Western legends. © Editions Dupuis.

Another noteworthy French Western of the Thirties is the unjustly neglected *L'Aigle des Montagnes Rocheuses* ("The Eagle of the Rocky Mountains") by Robert Dansler who, under his pseudonym of Bob Dan, also wrote countless Western novels. Like Marijac, Bob Dan was only a passable artist, but his eagle-nosed, square-jawed hero was well delineated, and his adventures, always entertaining, now exhibit a nostalgic charm.

In 1946 one of the most popular and successful of the French language Westerns made its debut: *Lucky Luke*, created by the talented cartoonist Morris (Maurice de Bevère). *Lucky Luke* is an affectionate take-off on the Western mythos, but its stories told only half tongue-in-cheek are also true to the very genre they purport to spoof. Thus Lucky Luke has tangled with crooked gamblers, horse thieves, psychopathic killers, and bank robbers, with suitable nonchalance. The last image of each adventure would show him riding into the sunset on his horse Jolly Jumper, while humming the self-deprecating refrain that made him famous: "I'm a poor lonesome cowboy . . ."

In 1955 the prolific René Goscinny, future creator of the world-acclaimed *Astérix*, joined Morris as *Lucky Luke*'s scriptwriter. Soon Goscinny peopled the strip with characters straight out of the real West: Judge Roy Bean "the law west of the Pecos," depicted as an unseemly bum addicted to moonshine, Jane Calamity represented as an ugly harridan, Billy the Kid, and Jesse James were all featured at one time or another. Goscinny's most hilarious creation was by far that of the four Dalton cousins, the hapless relatives of the dreaded Dalton brothers. If anything, Goscinny has a passion for authenticity. The plots and story lines may be outrageous, but the background details and settings are always painstakingly documented.

Of a far different character is Jijé's *Jerry Spring*, started in 1954 and still going strong, despite an interruption from 1967 to 1974. Jijé (Joseph Gillain) took all the hallowed conventions of the traditional Western but twisted them subtly into an allegory of life and death whose protagonists are the darkly handsome Jerry Spring and his juvenile Mexican companion, the cheerful and more pragmatic Poncho. Actually the idea of doing a Western had come to Jijé in the course of a long journey across the North-American continent. The innumerable sketches which the author drew during his American travels were to serve him well, and *Jerry Spring*'s authenticity and integrity come forcefully through.

Rising over the surface conventions of the plots which were usually scripted by others, Jijé has been

Jijé (Joseph Gillain), Jerry Spring. Rising over the surface conventions of the plot, Jijé has been able to convey the grandeur and harshness that are the West. © Editions Dupuis.

able to convey the grandeur and harshness that are the West; under his pen the magnificent vistas of the endless plains and forbidding deserts spring to life. The action, as ritual as in a kabuki play, takes on an added dimension of meaning and myth as the hero and the villains square off in their appointed roles as translucent as symbols; while the crowds of bystanders, idlers and fence straddlers, which Jijé delights in depicting, take on the unwitting role of a Greek chorus.

Among Jijé's admirers was his one-time assistant, Jean Giraud (Gir), who originated a Western of his own in 1963, *Fort Navajo* written by Jean-Michel Charlier, and later to be known as *Lieutenant Blueberry*. The strip's hero is a lieutenant of the post-Civil War U.S. Army named Mike Blueberry (actually Mike Donovan, a fugitive from justice framed on a murder charge), a strong-willed, non-conforming and hot-tempered roustabout, often at odds with his superiors. Blueberry is often assisted in his variegated endeavors by his grizzled sidekick, Jimmy McClure, an unreconstructed drunkard who shares the hero's fondness for whiskey, gambling and hell-raising.

The first episodes of the strip found Blueberry helping in the construction and defense of the transcontinental railway, and taking part in the campaigns against the Sioux. Of late our hero seems to have taken unofficial leave from the Army (where a good part of his time was spent in the stockade, anyway), and is currently engaging in free-lance activities of his own. Different and mysterious assignments have taken him variously to peace negotiations with the warring Navahos, in search of the lost Dutchman's mine in Arizona, and even down to old Mexico in hot pursuit of a band of desperadoes.

Lieutenant Blueberry is, without doubt, the most vigorous, exciting and refreshing Western since the early *Red Ryder*. It is also one of the most popular

Gir (Jean Giraud) and Jean-Michel Charlier, *Lieutenant Blueberry*. This strip is the most exciting Western since the early *Red Ryder*, and one of the most popular features in France. © Editions Dargaud.

comic strips in France, widely read and no less widely imitated.

Another Western strip of note to come out in recent times is *Comanche*, drawn by Hermann (Hermann Huppen) and written by Greg (Michel Régnier). If the adventures of the young and pretty ranch owner known as Comanche, her strong and taciturn foreman called Red Dust, and the comic old cow hand Ten Gallons, are more conventional than those of Mike Blueberry, they are always entertaining and often gripping.

Hermann and Greg (Hermann Huppen and Michel Régnier), *Comanche*. *Comanche* has reached the top among European comic strip Westerns, in popularity as well as in critical acclaim. © Editions du Lombard.

Greg's stories are well-researched and well-written, Hermann's style is sharp and forceful, and his compositions visually striking, with a bold use of color. Unlike *Blueberry*, *Comanche* sticks pretty close to its chosen locale, a sprawling cattle ranch in Wyoming. The depiction of familiar ranch scenes alternates with more violent episodes of thievery, skulduggery, murder and revenge. Since its inception in 1971, *Comanche* has reached the top among European comic strip Westerns, both in popularity and in critical acclaim.

As was stated earlier, Western strips in the French language are too numerous to mention. However, some of them deserve to be singled out here, either because of originality of theme or quality of draftsmanship. *Tom Mix*, the 1940 creation of François-Edmond Calvo, was only remotely based on the life of the fabled cowboy and movie star, but it was powerfully drawn and dramatically written. In the same vein, Buffalo Bill was also pictorialized in over a dozen different strips, most of them awful, from the Thirties to the present.

In recent times the Western has been flourishing in France and Belgium as never before, with such strips as *Buddy Longway*, the virile depiction of the lives of a white mountain man and his Indian wife by Derib; the excellent but unfortunately unfinished *Le Spécialiste* by Jijé; the picturesque and well-handled *Teddy Ted* by Gerald Forton; Lucien Nortier's imaginative account of the California gold rush days, *Sam Billie Bill;* and the unusual *Loup Noir* ("Black Wolf"), which tells the story of the West as seen through the eyes of a Sioux warrior.

The parodic Western is also well represented, with the very funny *Chick Bill* by Tibet (Gilbert Gascard), and *Les Tuniques Bleues* ("The Blue Coats"), an hilarious look at the goings-on in a U.S. outpost in the wild days of the frontier.

Westerns made in Italy

The "spaghetti Western" is not a recent innovation of Italian moviemakers. In point of fact the Italians have proved adept at turning out Westerns since the Thirties, at least on newspaper pages and in comic books. One of the earliest was *Ulceda* (1935) by the talented artist Guido Moroni-Celsi, about an Indian Princess, daughter of "the Great Hawk of the Prairies," and her love for an Italian adventurer. The most famous Italian Western of the Thirties, however, turned out to be *Kit Carson*, which first appeared in 1937.

Kit Carson was memorably written by Federico Pedrocchi who depicted the legendary frontier scout as a world-weary, fading figure of the Old West, whose ideals and fires still burned brightly under the gruff exterior. He was accompanied in his self-appointed rounds by the paunchy, slow-moving Uncle Pam, who played Sancho Panza to Kit's Don Quixote. The duo's adventures were filled with gunfights, ambushes, Indian attacks and outlaw raids. Pedrocchi's writing, literate and witty, was ably complemented by Rino Albertarelli's elegance of line. The graphic depiction of the epic battle between Kit Carson and a handful of U.S. infantrymen besieged in a lonely Army outpost on the one side, and the massed forces of the Sioux on the other, is still a masterpiece of action and suspense.

In 1939 Kit Carson, now drawn by the equally talented Walter Molino, moved south to Mexico, where he foiled the plans of the mad would-be dictator El Tuerto, and the equally nefarious schemes of the outlaw Carvajan, with the help of the mysterious "White Amazon." The series ended in 1940; it is now regarded as one of the classics of the Italian comic strip.

Derib, *Buddy Longway*. This strip depicts the tribulations of a mountain man and his Indian wife. © Editions du Lombard.

Jijé, *Le Spécialiste*. This spectacular Jijé Western has unfortunately remained uncompleted. © Jijé.

Salverius, *Les Tuniques Bleues*. Or an hilarious look at the goings on in a U.S. outpost in the wild days of the frontier. © Éditions Dupuis.

Walter Molino, *Kit Carson*. This outstanding Western strip is now regarded as one of the classics of the Italian comics. © Mondadori.

After the lull caused by World War II the Italian production of Westerns resumed unabated. In 1948 *Tex Willer*, written by Giovanni Bonelli and drawn by Aurelio Galleppini (Gallep), saw the light of print. Tex, as his name would indicate, is a Texas Ranger, a champion of justice and a righter of wrongs. A friend of the Navaho Indians, who have nicknamed him "Night Eagle," he is also the sworn enemy of outlaws, malefactors and other miscreants whom he pitilessly guns down in an unending succession of high noon confrontations. This series is much bloodier than any American Western, and its violence prefigures that of the later Western movies of Sergio Leone.

One of Tex's most constant companions in adventure turns out to be the afore-mentioned Kit Carson (obviously a popular Western figure in Italy) who often cools down the hot-tempered Ranger with his worldly and sagacious advice. Later Tex was joined by his own son, also named Kit, in homage to the Indian

Giovanni Bonelli and Aurelio Galleppini, *Tex Willer*. *Tex Willer* is a highly entertaining strip whose popularity has continued unabated since its inception in 1948. © Edizioni Araldo.

scout, who would learn the ropes at the side of his rough-riding father.

Tex Willer is a highly entertaining strip which sometimes oversteps the boundaries of the genre. Bonelli's imagination never flags, and he did not hesitate to veer away on occasions from purely Western themes to delve into science fiction, fantasy and even horror. His success has continued unabated for the last thirty years, so much so that Galleppini has had to call on a small army of assistants to help him in the task of drawing the adventures of the irrepressible Ranger. Those assistants have included Mario Uggeri, Erio Nicolo and Giovanni Ticci.

Pietro Gamba, *Pecos Bill*. A conventional Western built around the legendary Texas hero, *Pecos Bill* is not without merit. © Edizioni Alpe.

A host of Western strips followed hard on the heels of *Tex Willer*. One of the more brilliant, although not one of the more popular, was the short-lived *Kinowa* which appeared in comic book form in 1950. It told of the legend of Kinowa, "the Spirit of Evil," a mysterious figure of the night intent on bringing death to the blood-thirsty Indians of the Plains. In actuality Kinowa was a sun-crazed prospector named Sam Boyle who had been scalped by Indians when he was a youth and had vowed vengeance on all red men. When he donned the mask of the avenging demon, made even more terrifying by the campfire lights or the reflection of the moon, Sam was able to instill terror in the hearts of the Indians with his mere apparition. Ably written by Andrea Lavezzolo, and drawn by a number of different artists, *Kinowa* was a memorable and off-beat Western.

Kinowa had been preceded by a few months by another comic book horse-opera *Pecos Bill*, which proved more popular, lasting well into the Sixties. This was a more conventional Western, which told of the legendary exploits of the mythical Texas rider. Using his lariat as his only weapon, Pecos Bill was able to maintain order in the vast expanses of western Texas with a mixture of dexterity, swiftness, ubiquitousness, and fast thinking. His horse Turbine (Whirlpool) often was of invaluable assistance, his instincts warning the hero of impending danger or putting him on the trail of his quarry. Pecos Bill also had a sweetheart, the blonde, long-suffering Sue, but his heart throbbed for the guntoting, fiery Calamity Jane, who often shared his adventures. This is another instance of European artists mixing real and legendary figures of the West to good effect. A variety of writers and artists worked on *Pecos Bill* at one time or other, but the names of Raffaele Paparella, Dino Battaglia and Pietro Gamba (for the artwork), and Guido Martina (for the scripts) deserve to be singled out.

Of a far different character was *Il Piccolo Sceriffo* ("The Little Sheriff"), created (also in 1950) by Tristano Torelli and Dino Zuffi. This comic book, cheaply produced, poorly printed, and miserably drawn, nevertheless enjoyed a huge success among the younger readers. The hero was a teen-ager who had taken over the duties of his father, Sheriff Hodgkin, dastardly gunned down by a gang of outlaws; with the assistance of his sister, Lizzie, and of his pudgy companion, Piggie, the little sheriff helped bring law and order to the rampaging West. In spite of his young age he was able to outgun, outrun and outsmart any number of foes, be they bank robbers or Indian scalp-hunters. In the Sixties the hero was finally able

Tristano Torelli and Dino Zuffi, *Il Piccolo Sceriffo* ("The Little Sheriff"). © Dardo.

Benito Jacovitti, *Cocco Bill*. The satirical tone
of the dialogues and the outrageousness of
the situations have made *Cocco Bill*
outstanding among parodic Westerns.
© Corriere dei Ragazzi.

to grow up, and the strip was accordingly renamed *Il
Nuovo Sceriffo* ("The New Sheriff"). *Piccolo* or *Nuovo*,
however, this series has little to commend it, except
for its long-lasting popularity which is mainly due to
its legions of younger readers.

A later addition to the Western genre has been
Maschera Nera ("Black Mask"), which ran from 1962 to
1965. *Maschera Nera* was created by scriptwriter
Luciano Secchi, using the pen-name "Max Bunker,"
and artist Paolo Piffarerio. *Maschera Nera* was a
Zorro-type avenger concealing under his mask the
identity of Ringo Rowandt, a European-educated
lawyer, the son of the local sheriff. Among the cast

were a number of colorful characters such as the uncouth Judge Colt, intrigued by Ringo's speech and manners; Mister Full, the gambler; and Larry Small, the deputy sheriff and Ringo's rival for the love of the beautiful Wilma Morrison. Maschera Nera's foes have been many, from the deadly Gang of the Owl to the "Ivory Totem," the master of disguise and deception.

Italy has also produced its own entry in the flourishing subgenre of the parodic Western: the outrageous and rib-splitting *Cocco Bill* by Benito Jacovitti. Originated in 1957 it is still running at this writing. One of the most endearing of mock-epic Western heroes, Cocco Bill is a heavy drinker of camomile tea and a teetotaller. He is endowed with more than his share of virtues and attributes: uncommonly strong and courageous, handy with his guns as well as with his fists, he can also out-talk any man alive or dead. The satirical tone of the dialogues and the outlandishness of the situations have made *Cocco Bill* outstanding in a field that is rapidly becoming overcrowded and overplayed.

Italian Westerns have been tumbling out of the comic pages in seemingly inexhaustible numbers. There have been *Bufalo Bill* (spelled with one "f"), created in 1951 by Luigi Grecchi and Carlo Cossio, a fanciful version of the Indian scout and show-biz entrepreneur's lives and times; *I Tre Bill* ("The Three Bills"), about the exploits of three brothers in Old Arizona; *Capitan Miki*, another juvenile Western; *Yuma Kid*, admirably drawn by Mario Uggeri; *Kirbi Flint*, a mature horse-opera well written by Sergio Tuis and drawn in loving detail by Antonio Canale; and *Mani in Alto!* ("Hands Up!"), an unusual strip by Rinaldo d'Ami (signing "Roy D'Amy"), with a motley cast of characters straight out of grade-B Western movies.

In the traditionally male preserve of the Western the female cartoonist Lina Buffolente has carved out a niche of her own with such diverse cowboy features as

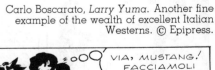

Carlo Boscarato, *Larry Yuma*. Another fine example of the wealth of excellent Italian Westerns. © Epipress.

Lina Buffolente, *Jane Calamity*. The figure of the legendary Calamity Jane was bound to attract the attention of Lina Buffolente, one of the very few women cartoonists working in the Western genre. © Lina Buffolente.

Frisco Jim, Colorado Kid, Tom Mix (yet another version!), *Liberty Kid,* and *Il Piccolo Ranger* ("The Little Ranger") an obvious answer to "The Little Sheriff". Buffolente has also taken advantage of her position to strike a blow for women's rights with her spirited depiction of that legendary Western heroine, *Jane Calamity,* as Calamity Jane is commonly known in Italy.

From merry England to sunny Spain

The British started turning to adventure—and Western—themes in the mid-Thirties. Reg Perrott, one of England's most gifted strip artists, created (in 1936) *White Cloud,* an atmospheric Indian tale set in the 1880's, followed (in March 1939) by *Red Rider,* a Western adventure not too dissimilar from Fred Harman's *Red Ryder.* A showdown at high noon between the two rival cowpunchers was barely avoided when Perrott enlisted in the Royal Air Force at the outbreak of World War II and dropped the strip. Perrott went back to comics after the war, but no other Western came out of his facile pen before his untimely death around 1948.

Perrott's most prolific rival on the Western scene was undoubtedly George Heath who, in the space of two years (1934-36), spun out no fewer than three different Western yarns, *Red Man's Gold, Fortune in the Desert,* and *Call of the West,* strongly inspired by current American movie serials. In 1936 he was again back with *Tim McCoy,* a strip adaptation of the Western star's screen adventures. In the late Forties and early Fifties Heath was to originate two more Westerns, *Outlaw Trail* and *Cowboy Charlie,* both mediocre and both short-lived.

By the late Thirties there was such a proliferation of British horse-operas that parody was inevitable. Actually there had been Western spoofs as early as the Twenties, but these satirized Western movies of the silent era, and were usually short, self-contained pieces such as Reg Parlett's *Sheriff of Sherbet City,* or his brother George Parlett's *Prairie Pranks.* Things started in earnest (if that's the right word) with *Desperate Dan.*

Dudley D. Watkins, *Desperate Dan.* An odd mixture of Western lore and traditional British humor, *Desperate Dan* has remained popular through the years. © Dandy.

Desperate Dan was the 1937 creation of Dudley D. Watkins. Its hero's official "biography" started with these words: "Desperate Dan was born in the town of Tombstone, and all the natives of that town are tough, but Desperate Dan was the toughest of all." A cowboy endowed with super-human abilities, Dan lived up to his reputation by demolishing those saloons where he felt service was not fast enough, or flattening a whole bunch of rival cowpokes with a single flick of the wrist. Later he settled in Cactusville where he became the bane of any evildoer that ever chanced thattaway. *Desperate Dan* is an odd mixture of mock Western lore and quaint British touches; Cactusville, for instance, is noted for its Victorian lampposts and its addiction to cricket! It is a very funny as well as a highly popular comic strip which is still running to this day.

Geoff Campion, *Billy The Kid*. The hero bore no resemblance to the historical Billy, but was a Western Robin Hood forever fighting against injustice. © Amalgamated Press.

The Fifties probably marked the high point of popularity for Western strips in Britain. In 1952 Geoff Campion started *Billy the Kid*, whose hero bore more than passing resemblance to movie star Robert Taylor who had impersonated the Kid on screen in the 1941 version, and no historical resemblance whatever to William Bonney, the real Billy the Kid. As depicted by Campion, Billy was a latter-day Robin Hood, defending widows and orphans against the manipulations of unscrupulous robber barons and their accomplices hiding behind the law. He was clearly patterned on the Lone Ranger, even down to the Kid's battle cry: "Yip! yip! yip! Hi-yo!"

Ron Embleton, *The Lone Star Rider*. *The Lone Star Rider* was another good example of the British Westerns that flourished during the Fifties. © Atlas.

On the same general theme there was created in 1952 a comic book series titled *The Lone Star Rider*. Its hero, Steve Larabee, was again a lone horseman, whose non-human companions were his horse Smoky and his dog Pagan. The scripts were often muddled, and the drawing, while competent, was not on a par with the excellent draftsmanship of the rival *Billy the Kid*. Started as a promotional giveaway for the Die Cast Metal Tools Company, the comic book was later taken over by its distributor, Atlas, and enjoyed a fairly good run into the Sixties.

Among the many hands who drew *The Lone Star Rider* the most distinctive was unquestionably that of Ron Embleton, one of the best Western illustrators of the period. Among the many Westerns to Embleton's credit, mention should be made of *Black Hawk* (a 1948 one-shot), of *Big Indian* (1948-49), and especially of the excellent and realistically documented *Mohawk Trail* (1951-52).

So popular was the American West with British readers that it gave rise to a great number of specialized comic books. The same trend, as we have seen, was also evident in the United States at the time. These publications bore such names as *Western Super Thriller Comics, Western Star Comics, Cowboy Comics,* and *Cowboy Action.* Some were reprints of American titles, but many carried original material. The most entertaining of those was *Western War Comics* which devoted itself to the exploits of such divergent historical figures as Kit Carson, Daniel Boone and Crazy Horse.

Harry Bishop, *Gun Law.* Based on TV's long-lived *Gunsmoke* series, this strip displays a far more uninhibited approach than its screen inspiration. © Daily Express.

The Sixties saw the creation of *Gun Law* by Harry Bishop. Its hero was none other than the most famous U.S. marshal of all time, our friend Matt Dillon, of Dodge City. In fact the strip is an almost exact replica of the *Gunsmoke* TV series, complete with Miss Kitty, Chester (and later Festus), Doc, and all the familiar characters hanging around the Long Branch saloon. The plots are sometimes lifted whole from the TV scripts, sometimes original (and considerably sexier); the protagonists, however, are fashioned faithfully after the likes of Jim Arness, Amanda Blake, or Milburn Stone.

The success of *Gun Law* has been so great that it soon gave rise to a competitor, Tony Weare's *Matt Mariott,* whose two-fisted title character pursues his adventures in the London *Daily Mail* while *Gun Law* runs in the rival *Daily Express.* In Britain, as in the rest of Europe, the Western tradition remains as solid as ever. England's most gifted comic strip artist, Frank Bellamy, had started a Western feature of his own, *Swade,* just months before his untimely death in 1976.

This popularity manifests itself even in Germany where Western strips (and comic strips in general) have long been held in suspicion. Best representative of this new spirit of acceptance is the immensely popular *Winnetou* series.

MATT MARRIOTT
by TONY WEARE
& JAMES EDGAR

THE INDIANS PULL BACK

RUNNING BEAR IS DEAD, WHITE EAGLE. I SAW IT FROM THE PALISADE. BUT FIRST HE KILLED THE WHITE MAN HILLYARD

THEN WHY DO WE FIGHT!

OUR LEADER IS DEAD AND THE MAN HE SOUGHT IS DEAD. WE WILL PARLEY WITH DEVLIN

SO LET THERE BE NO MORE TALK OF FIGHTING. COLLECT YOUR DEAD AND GO BACK WITH HONOUR TO YOUR LODGES

Tony Weare, *Matt Mariott*. The Western tradition remains as solid as ever in London newspapers. © Daily Mail.

Based on the novels of Karl May, an incredible writer whose books were once accepted as true documents of the American West, although May had never set foot on the New Continent, the strip began its long career in 1963. It tells of the friendship between the frontier scout Old Shatterhand and the Apache chief Winnetou. The action is full of blood and thunder, of epic battles between the Apaches and the Kiowas, between the righteous Indians and the white carpetbaggers trying to steal their land, etc. The West depicted in *Winnetou* is almost entirely fictional. Even the geography and chronology are often in flagrant error, but it does convey some flavor of the rough, albeit glamorized, life on the wild Prairie.

The artwork on the *Winnetou* strip has been done by a variety of hands (Juan Arranz, Walter Neugebauer, cartoonists of the Vandersteen studio, etc.) but only Helmut Nickel has been able to translate into graphic terms the fascination conveyed by the May novels.

Helmut Nickel, *Winnetou*. Based on Karl May's popular novels, *Winnetou* is Germany's most successful Western strip. © Walter Lehning Verlag.

Hansrudi Wäscher, *Buffalo Bill*. One among the countless comic strip versions of the career of the fabled Colonel Cody, this German feature is also one of the more entertaining. © Bastei Verlag.

Another German Western of interest is *Buffalo Bill*. This umpteenth comic strip version of the real and supposed exploits of the fabled Colonel Cody was begun, as were so many other German comic strips, in the Dutch studio of Willy Vandersteen in 1968. It has since then known an almost endless succession of artists, including Raul Sola and Hansrudi Wäscher. This German-produced *Buffalo Bill* is probably one of the most outlandish depictions of Cody's career although it does have strong competition in some of the versions published in Italy and France: the hero can be seen bringing down a Sioux uprising almost single-handedly, or helping build the transcontinental railway.

Buffalo Bill and *Winnetou* are only two of the Western strips currently being published in Germany. In fact the Western genre is so strong that it was possible for a German publisher to bring out a weekly comic book, *Lasso*, entirely devoted to Western adventure with such features as the American *Reno Kid*, and reprints from the U.S., Argentina and several European countries.

The Dutch, who have contributed so much of the German Western fare, have also produced a number of features for home consumption. The Netherlands' most talented cartoonist, Hans G. Kresse, has been responsible for quite a few of those, including *De Avonturen van Tom Texan* ("The Adventures of Tom Texan," 1940-41), *Matho Tonga*, and *Zorro*.

Kresse's most ambitious project saw the light of print in 1972, when he began his series *De Indianen* ("The Indians"). It is the artist's intent to retrace the history of the North American Indians from the time of the Spanish conquest to the present, through the vi-

Hans G. Kresse, *De Indianen*. This ambitious series aims at recreating the history of the North American Indians from the time of the Spanish conquest up to the present. © Hans G. Kresse.

Andrija Maurović, *Stari Mačak* ("The Old Cat"). This original Western strip was one of the earliest Yugoslav comics. © Andrija Maurović.

cissitudes of a fictional family, part of the Apache nation. The first episodes told of Chaka, the head of the clan, and his two sons, Unda and Anúa, and their fight against the Spanish invaders moving north from Mexico. With the help of Mestizo, the half-breed, Chaka and his clan are able to outwit and outfight the Spaniards, whom the Indians call "the masters of the thunder," because of their use of firearms. After the opening sequences, the action has now shifted away from Chaka to his son Anúa in what promises to be a long, exciting, and original saga of the American West.

In complement to the action, Kresse has regularly been drawing vignettes of authentic Indian life and lore, including some incredibly detailed renderings of costumes, dwellings, hunting scenes and religious rituals.

No European country has proved immune to the call of the West. For instance, Andrija Maurović who is called the father of the Yugoslav comic strip created *Stari Mačak* ("The Old Cat") in 1937, a strip about an aging gunfighter who could still outdraw and outrun opponents half his age. The feature soon became the most popular and successful of all comic strips in Yugoslavia, and only disappeared because of the war. In 1968 Maurović tried to revive his hero in *Povratak Starog Mačak* ("The Return of the Old Cat"), but the sequel was not a success.

Like her Latin sisters, France and Italy, Spain has also been a great upholder of the Western myth. Spain's Western production may have started later than those of Italy and France, but this was more than offset by the number and quality of the Western features she has been turning out.

The first horse-opera of note to come out of Spain was *Pistol Jim*, introduced in October 1945 to Spanish readers by Carlos Freixas. The feature actually had originated in Argentina a few months earlier. Pistol Jim was unabashedly patterned after the cowboy heroes of Republic and Paramount movie series. He always dressed in black attire like Hopalong Cassidy, and, adorned with a six-shooter on his shirt front, he would cheerfully embark on any dangerous assignment that came his way, from putting an end to the depredations of a gang of bank robbers to rescuing an heiress from the clutches of her kidnappers. As was the custom of the day, Pistol Jim had a youthful sidekick in the person of a freckled-faced urchin named Nick Rolly, and he was the reluctant object of the affections of two ladies: the "good" Nelly Cayo, a wealthy (and sexy) ranch owner, and the "bad" Belle Smith, a saloon singer with a past, whose advances our hero sometimes found hard to resist. Belle Smith once dragged Pistol Jim into her room where she bluntly declared: "You're a man according to my heart. We could be great friends . . . let me see you without your hat . . ."

Despite its promises, *Pistol Jim* lasted only for one year, disappearing in October 1946.

Carlos Freixas, *Pistol Jim*. Pistol Jim is a good example of Spanish Western comics. © Carlos Freixas.

Hard on the heels of *Pistol Jim* came *El Coyote*, adapted in 1946 from the popular novels of José Mallorquí into comic book form. El Coyote was a Zorro-type avenger, in actuality the young and wealthy ranch owner Don Cesar de Echagüe, who donned black costume and mask to wreak retribution upon the *yanqui* soldiers and the desperadoes who were despoiling northern Mexico at the time of the Mexican-American war.

The *El Coyote* comic books were at first drawn by Francisco Batet, who had previously illustrated Mallorquí's novels. Batet's version, while commendable, suffered from a surfeit of verbosity: he would, for instance, add lengthy narratives to illustrations that were fully self-explanatory. His depiction of the masked hero, however, was faultless: the mustachoed, sombrero-hatted Coyote, whose eyes could

Francisco Batet, *El Coyote*. Inspired by José Mallorquí's novels, *El Coyote* soon became Spain's most popular strip. © Ediciones Cliper.

be seen burning fiercely under the mask, was made into a credible avenging angel by Batet's restless, compelling line. Some of the villains were also memorable, particularly the horrible couple of Gimoteo and his disfigured wife.

In the Forties *El Coyote* was among the most popular comic books in Spain, with countless reprintings, and a clamoring coterie of fans. When Batet moved to France in the Fifties the feature was taken over by José Ramon Larraz who proved far less inspired (or clever) than his predecessor.

In 1963 Carlos Giménez, who had cut his teeth illustrating a number of *Buck Jones* comic books published in France, originated *Gringo* on a script by Manuel Medina.

Gringo was a boyish, fair-haired American cowboy whose real name was Syd Viking. His nickname had been given to him by the Mexican ranch hands jealous of his young age and blond good looks; he had proudly accepted the appellation and, by dint of innumerable feats of valor and skill, had turned it into a term of admiration and affection. In the beginning Gringo was foreman of a cattle ranch, but he soon followed the trail blazed by countless comic strip and movie cowboys before him—he took to the open spaces in no time and became one more knight errant of the plains, always ready to lend his gun to a just and noble cause.

Giménez, who is now regarded as one of Spain's foremost cartoonists, left the strip after a while, and has since been succeeded by a horde of different artists, Domingo Alvarez Lopez and Suso (Jesús Peña Rego) notable among them.

In recent times there has been a greater and greater attraction for the Western among the Spanish public. Some noted cartoonists have accordingly tried their

Carlos Giménez, *Gringo*. Another Western made in Spain, *Gringo* was graced with Giménez's elegant penwork. © Selecciones Illustradas.

Antonio Hernandez Palacios, *Manos Kelly*.
Manos Kelly is a masterful Spanish Western
of recent vintage. © Trinca.

hands at the genre. Perhaps one of the most strikingly handsome of modern Western strips from any country is *Manos Kelly*, masterfully drawn since 1970 by Antonio Hernandez Palacios. Presented as a former guide to General Winfield Scott (in fiction if not in fact) at the time of the Guadalupe treaty of 1848, Kelly later left the Army and pursued a wandering life of adventure. A witness to the California gold rush and the wagon train era, he is also a participant in the struggles pitting landowners against squatters, prospectors against claim-jumpers, white settlers against the dispossessed Indians. A defender of the weak and the oppressed, Manos Kelly's life is as lonely as it is dangerous.

In addition to its taut, nervous scripts, *Manos Kelly* is also noted for Hernandez's artistry, his sense of composition, and his dark, brooding landscapes which reflect the inner conflicts of the hero.

Another example of the latter-day psychological Western is *Los Guerilleros* created in 1968 by the noted cartoonist Jesús Blasco for the Belgian magazine *Spirou*, and now published in Spanish magazines as well. Actually Blasco is no stranger to the Western genre. He had been drawing horse operas since the late Forties, with such short-lived creations as *Wild Batson*, *Smiley O'Hara*, and *En los Dominios de los Sioux* ("In the Land of the Sioux"), and he had also been a contributor to such foreign titles as *Billy the Kid*, *Wyatt Earp*, *Buffalo Bill*, *Blackbow* and *Shot Basky*. When he started *Los Guerilleros*, Blasco's style was therefore well established.

The story revolves around the friendship of a trio of adventurers: the young American, strong and chivalrous, named Ray; Yuma, the resourceful and wily Apache; and the coarse, shabby and disreputable

Jesús Blasco, *Los Guerilleros*. Blasco's comic feature originated in Belgium but is now published in Spain. © Éditions Dupuis.

Pedro de Guzman. Blasco's draftsmanship is striking, his compositions a trifle too elaborate, but eye-catching nonetheless. His scripts, however, are obscure. It is often hard to follow all the twists of the plot, and the motivations of the protagonists often seem muddle-headed. They are guerilleros, indeed, but their unremitting war against ruthless land barons, unscrupulous Indian agents and rapacious speculators appears at times pointless, and at other times downright offensive.

The West (north, south and east)

It is a geographical fact that the American West does not stop at the Rio Grande or the Canadian border; and there is accordingly a Western tradition in both Canada and Mexico, however different it may be from ours.

The Canadian West has always been symbolized in the eyes of the rest of the world by the dashing troopers of the Royal Mounted Police. It is therefore not surprising to find one of the rare Canadian strips from a newspaper of the Thirties devoted to the exploits of the legendary Mounties. Fittingly called *Men of the Mounted* it was created in 1936 by writer Ted McCall and artist Harry Hall for the *Toronto Telegram*. Afflicted with ponderous scripts and mediocre artwork, it did not hold a candle to the American *King of the Royal Mounted* and disappeared with the decade.

Ted McCall and Harry Hall, *Men of the Mounted*. © Toronto Telegram.

PEERING through the small window high up on the Strange Chateau, Corporal Keene shouted in rage when he saw O'Hara, helpless, attacked by the brutal Ling . . . He climbed through the window with blazing eyes . . .

For a brief instant the Corporal and Ling faced each other like gladiators of old . . . Slowly the Chinese drew a knife . . . "The Corporal!" he whispered. "Delivered into my hands!" . . . A grim smile spread over the Mountie's face . . .

"For what you have done to O'Hara," he ground out in a deadly voice, "you'll pay . . . and pay now!" . . . He sprang at the waiting Oriental, twisting aside to escape the gleaming knife that slashed at him like lightning . . .

The Chinese screamed as the knife missed its mark . . . Then the Corporal was on him, lashing at him like a man gone mad, pounding with a fury that demanded vengeance for the scores of victims of this Oriental arch-criminal . . .

E.T. Legault, *Dixon of the Mounted.* All through the years the "Mountie" has remained a popular staple of Canadian comic strips. © Active Comics.

Another try at the Mountie theme was *Dixon of the Mounted* by the French-Canadian cartoonist E.T. Legault. Started as one in a series of black-and-white comic books (the so-called "Canadian whites") in the Forties, when the wartime paper shortage had severely curtailed the import of American comic books, it was an undistinguished effort and did not survive the war.

Somewhat better drawn and written, but just as short-lived, was *Larry Brannon*, another Mountie feature originated in 1960 by Winslow Mortimer. Brannon bore a definite resemblance to Sergeant King but, if anything, his adventures were even faster. This effort came at a time of rising disaffection for the adventure strip, however, and its promises were never fullfilled.

Mexico has had better luck in establishing the Western as a respected genre in comic books and newspapers. The Westerns made in Mexico have been almost equally divided between stories with a Mexican locale and those taking place in the United States; those strips grounded in Mexican tradition or folklore have uniformally (and predictably) proven to be more popular and longer lasting.

Adolfo Mariño Ruiz, *El Charro Negro*. *El Charro Negro* ("The Black Rider") was an early Mexican Western of note. © Paquin.

As in many other countries around the world, Mexican cartoonists did not start producing Western features before the Thirties. Among the early titles worthy of notice one should mention *Águila Roja* ("Red Eagle") created by Leopoldo Zea Salas in 1936, the story of a frontier lawman who used his lariat in preference to his guns; and *El Charro Negro* ("The Black Rider"). This latter feature, created in 1937 by Adolfo Mariño Ruiz, was notable for its elegant draftsmanship, its loving depiction of the Mexican landscape, and its far-fetched, but entertaining, story-lines. It was the most popular comic strip in Mexico all through the late Thirties and early Forties. Also in 1937 Abel Quezada originated *Maximo Tops* which related, in a tone half-parodic and half-serious, the tribulations of a red-haired, freckle-faced, two-fisted sheriff. The same humorous mood prevailed in Antonio Campuzano Oñate's fittingly named *Rancho Alegre* ("Merry Ranch"), about a sombrero-hatted Mexican adventurer and his kid-companion Pedrito.

Of more modern vintage, two Mexican comic books are especially worthy of notice. The first one is *Alma Grande* ("Big Soul"), created in 1961 by the writer/artist team of Pedro Zapiain and José Suarez Lozano. The featured hero, Alma Grande, dubbed "the justice-fighting Yaqui," is a half-breed Yaqui Indian who battles for freedom and fairness to the *peones*, and against the rapacious landowners who exploit them. His enemies are the venomous Colonel Venegas, the representative of dictatorial order, the wealthy land-holder Count Cieza, and Laura, the Colonel's beautiful but lethal daughter. In his endeavors Alma Grande is assisted by a trio of friends, the taciturn Swede, the disquieting Culebra Prieta (Black Serpent), and the youthful Marcelino. Also a help (and sometimes a hindrance) is Alma Grande's fiancée, Alice the schoolteacher.

The tone of this class-conscious comic book is truly epic, with a whole rogue's gallery of antagonists, an endless succession of chases on horseback, fires, abductions, brawls and gunfights, and tight, skillfully plotted scripts built round a strong central theme, that of the eternal fight between justice and oppression, ignorance and light.

Much less ambitious in its design but even more popular in its appeal is *El Payo* ("The Towhead"), started in 1965. A weekly comic book carrying the subtitle "A Man Against the World," *El Payo* was created by writer Guillermo Vigil, with Fausto Buendía, Jr. as his first illustrator. The action is centered around the fictional little town of Vilmayo, in northern Mexico, although El Payo's adventures have ranged far and wide in typical Western tradition. The stories are an ingenious admixture of violence and sex, with El Payo fighting it out alone against assorted gangs of toughs, bandits and warlords, in order to save some innocent (and sexy) young girl from a fate worse than death. Although the hero seems to live in almost explicit concubinage with his girlfriend, the fiery Lupita, he easily succumbs to the advances from his uniformly grateful damsels out of distress.

José Suarez Lozano, *Alma Grande*. Subtitled "the justice-fighting Yaqui," *Alma Grande* is a class-conscious Western. © Novedades.

EL FUEGO YAQUI DETUVO EN SECO LA HUÍDA DE LOS BANDIDOS.

¡YUUUJJJAAAYYY!

BUCUM   BUCUM

CONOCÍAN LOS TORMENTOS QUE AYAKO DABA A LOS QUE SE DEJABAN ATRAPAR VIVOS...Y LO ARRIESGARON TODO EN SU AFÁN DE HUIR.

In spite of criticism leveled against its sensationalism and violence, *El Payo* remains an excellent example of its kind, and it often rivals in imagination and zest the best American comic books published in the same genre.

Guillermo Vigil and Fausto Buendía, *El Payo*. *El Payo* is a modern Western mixing action and sex. © Editorial Senda.

The Argentinians have long had their own brand of Western, depicting the hard life of the pampas, and the exploits of the gauchos, celebrated in story and song. These in turn have found an echo in such comic strips as *El Tigre de los Llanos*, *Fuerte Argentina*, *El Huinca*, *Lindor Covas*, and countless others. Yet so strong has been the lure of the North American West that a long and distinguished tradition of Western strips has been established in the land of the gauchos.

Just as in many of the other countries the trend started in the Thirties. The first such Western seems to have been the 1931 creation of José Vidal Davila, *Douglas Watson*. The hero was a Canadian Mountie, perhaps representing the height of exoticism for Argentine readers. The strip was rather undistinguished, with poor draftsmanship and mediocre stories set in type underneath the pictures. Raúl Roux's *Buffalo Bill* (every country seems to have had at least one shot at that particular hero) was somewhat better drawn but did not last. Another interesting Western creation of the Thirties was *El Rey de las Praderas* ("The King of the Prairies") by Enrique Rapela who later became one of the most gifted practioners of the "gauchesca" (gaucho story). Finally let us mention the comic strip adaptation of *The Last of the Mohicans* by the then-fledgling cartoonist José-Luis Salinas, who would go on to greater heights of draftsmanship with his masterful *Cisco Kid*.

One of the most off-beat as well as one of the best Westerns to come out of Argentina was *Sgt. Kirk*, created in 1953 by the prolific writer and editor Héctor Oesterheld. The title character was a deserter from the U.S. Army who lived among his friends, the Indians of the Plains, and whom his creator has described in these words: "Kirk lives in the world of the "tepee," he is a part of it and he knows the Indian as a brother ... And he also lives in the cowboy world, that of the horse, the saloon, the gunfights. Tormented by his renegade role, Kirk is an embittered hero, but friendship is his salvation." The strip was

José Vidal Davila, *Douglas Watson*. An early Argentine Western with a Canadian Mountie as hero. © Mustafá.

Hugo Pratt, *Sgt. Kirk*. This excellent Western was originated in Argentina by Italian cartoonist Hugo Pratt. © Editorial Abril.

drawn by the Italian cartoonist Hugo Pratt, then living in Argentina, who turned *Sgt. Kirk* into his first acknowledged masterwork.

The first episode recounts how the hero, sickened by the massacre of peaceful Indians at Pueblo Negro, decides to desert from the Army and join the Tchattooga tribe. Later he would meet his two most trusted friends, the young Indian brave Maha, and the understanding Dr. Forbes. The scenes of battles, of charges, of deadly encounters are extremely well depicted by Pratt, who also excels in the epic recreation of the world of the Western frontier, a man's world where women seldom appear.

Arturo Del Castillo, *Randall. Randall* is a Western in the classic mold transformed by Del Castillo into an allegorical epic. © Frontera.

Two other Oesterheld Westerns of distinction came out during this same period: the rambling, sprawling *Ticonderoga*, also drawn by Pratt in which the action is set in the late 18th century, and the more traditional *Verdugo Ranch*, excellently drawn by Pavone. Towering over all of them, however, was *Randall*, begun in 1957, and illustrated by Arturo Del Castillo, probably Latin America's most accomplished draftsman, along with Salinas.

Randall is a Western in the classic mold, but transformed by Del Castillo into an allegorical epic of monumental dimensions. A former soldier in the Union army, Randall embodies the modern type of knight errant, forever pursuing his mission of justice in the vast and lonely expanses of the post-Civil War West. A traditional, even well-worn, theme, made

Hiroshi Hirata, *Katume no Gunshi* ("The One-Eyed Officer"). The Japanese have adopted the Western genre and made it into their own, with samurai warriors playing the roles of the traditional cowboys, in what is called "jidaimono." © Hiroshi Hirata.

familiar by countless movies, which is here given fresh impetus by Del Castillo's ample, incisive and always kinetic style of drawing. The artist's compositions are more like choreographed sequences, with the hero performing his ritual dance of valor in the midst of his enemies, and objects and scenery simply—sometimes even abstractly—sketched in the background as mere props to the action.

The Japanese, with their peculiar blend of nationalism and pragmatism, have adopted the Western genre and remade it into their own, with samurai warriors playing the role of the traditional cowboys, in what is called "jidaimono." How close the jidaimono comes to the good old-fashioned Western can be seen, for instance, in Kurosawa's film epic, *The Seven Samurai*, itself later adapted with the greatest of ease into the movie Western, *The Magnificent Seven*. (In the same vein Kurosawa's *Yojimbo* formed the basis of the spaghetti Western, *For a Fistful of Dollars*.) Yet, even in Japan, some of the best cartoonists have tried their hand at a Western or two, like Osamu ("The King") Tezuka with his *Lemon Kid* (sic) and Sanpei Shirato with *Shinigami Shōnen Kim* "Kim's Momentous Adventures").

These were short-lived creations, however, mere exercises for Tezuka and Shirato on their way to greater things. The only Japanese Western that can be ranked among the productions of the United States, Italy, France, or Argentina, is *Daiheigenji* ("A Boy of the Western Plains"), which appeared in 1950.

This was a conventional Western, whose hero, Daiheigenji Jim, became an orphan when his parents were slain by the dreaded King Hell gang. Brought up to become a fearless gunfighter and horse rider, Daiheigenji used his talents to avenge his parents' deaths and rid the West of King Hell and his outlaws. Daiheigenji also battled the Apaches as well as a bevy of villains and villainesses sporting such colorful names as Red Bear and Wolf Girl. In his endeavors he was assisted by the enigmatic chief of the Chitseputsu tribe, Tomahawk Morgan, and by Jane, a fugitive from justice. *Daiheigenji* was written and drawn in a hard-hitting style by Shigeru Komatsuzaki, one of Japan's more accomplished draftsmen.

Daiheigenji provides a fitting finale to this chapter. From the Far West to the Far East what can be more symbolic of the universality of a myth that has transcended all national boundaries and all ethnic cultures?

One note in conclusion: it might seem paradoxical to see the Western strip flourish in all parts of the world while it is slowly dying in America. The answer, of course, lies in the sad fact that the American newspaper strips have almost completely abandoned adventure and action, while the comic books have never been able to shake the super-hero hang-up; on the other hand, Europeans and Latin Americans look upon the Western as a modern allegory of the eternal struggle between good and evil, and see in the lone cowboy the rightful heir of the wandering knight of medieval epics and novels of chivalry.

CHAPTER FIVE

THEMES AND INSPIRATIONS

© Epipress

In the course of their already long history, the Western comics have drawn their inspiration as well as their themes from a variety of sources. The primary source was, of course, the land itself, the Garden of the West, majestic and unchangeable despite the inroads of modern civilization and desecration. The peaks and forests of the Rockies, the sands and canyons of the Southwestern deserts, have become part of the American consciousness as a state of mind, an object of desire, as well as the symbol of a vanished and longed for wilderness.

The taming of this land, the *conquest* of the West, is of course part and parcel of American legend as well as history. A large segment of American literature has been devoted, sometimes obsessively, to the single theme of the frontier. Washington Irving's *A Tour of the Prairies*, Fenimore Cooper's Leatherstocking saga were first to blaze a fertile trail followed by such luminaries as Bret Harte and Mark Twain, all the way to the novels of Owen Wister, Luke Short, Zane Grey and Louis L'Amour. The literary tradition has been accompanied by a no less fecund pictorialization of the West; Frederic Remington and Charles Russell are the most celebrated Western artists, but the genre is still going strong and thriving. It is useful to note at this juncture that many comic strip artists have been contributing to the immortalization of the West in art, including Fred Harman, Vic Forsythe, J. R. Williams and James Swinnerton.

It is the purpose of this chapter to trace the more obvious influences and references, as they are reflected in Western comics, and to show how in turn the artists of the comics have treated the traditional themes and situations of the West.

The land

The most instantly recognizable feature of any Western is its setting. The familiar landscapes of the West help establish not only a sense of place, but a mood and a feeling of expectation; they are charged with meaning—half history, half symbol—a meaning far outweighing that of any other geographical place in the minds of western man. They are the equivalent of the alternately stark and luminous backgrounds depicting Heaven and Hell in medieval morality plays.

Of course some comic strips have dwelled on the emotional appeal of the Western landscape more deeply than others, according to the design and knowledge of their authors. A modern strip such as *Tumbleweeds* makes only minimal use of backgrounds, revealing itself by this single instance as being closer to the stylized mode of such features as *Peanuts* or *B.C.* than to the traditional Western. On the other hand the no less contemporary *Rick O'Shay* lovingly details the infinite variety and moods of the Western landscape, reflecting the deep knowledge and intimate concern of its author, Stan Lynde, himself a cattle rancher in Montana.

Fred Harman's working knowledge of the West has already been amply documented in a previous chapter, but stress should be given to the uneventful interludes in which the author allows his hero, Red Ryder, to reflectively pause in the course of the action, and lovingly gaze upon the awesome vistas of the western land. *Red Ryder* is thus incontrovertably shown as a paean to the West as much as a tale of adventure.

The trend is even more glaringly exposed in the two comic strips directly derived from Zane Grey's inspiration (if not always from his pen), *Tex Thorne* and *King of the Royal Mounted*. Time and again the two heroes,

Alex Raymond, magazine illustration. Alex Raymond, better known for *Flash Gordon* and *Rip Kirby*, was among the many cartoonists who tried their hand at Western illustration.

Tex of the southern plains, King of the northern climes, are depicted as small, almost forlorn, figures dwarfed by the majesty of the primeval earth. There is in a 1938 *King* sequence ("The Treasure of Malo the Hunter") a lyrical passage during which the hero travels the whole length of the Garden of the West from the outlying town through the verdant plains all the way to the icy wastelands of the Arctic Circle—and then back. The resemblance to many songs from the medieval epics (*Launcelot of the Lake* and *The Romance of the Rose*, notably) is too striking to be accidental.

There is the same feeling of reverence and awe in most European Westerns. The hallucinatory presence of the untamed wilderness contributed to the success of *Jim Boum* more than any elements of plot or situation. In the same vein the land plays a major if less overwhelming role in *Lieutenant Blueberry*, *Comanche*, *Winnetou* or *Tex Willer*. Gir is especially adept at delineating the tortured crags and contours of an inhospitable earth, while Hermann's inspiration is more elegiac, and its depiction of the Wyoming grazing lands more graceful than forbidding.

Stan Lynde, *Rick O'Shay*. The scenery forms an important part of *Rick O'Shay*'s appeal.
© Chicago Tribune-New York News Syndicate.

Fred Harman, *Red Ryder*. A reflective pause in the action of the strip. © NEA Service.

On the other hand a strip like *The Lone Ranger* made only sparse use of the scenery of the West, perhaps reflecting its radio show origins. This paucity of backgrounds strongly detracted from the action, which always seemed unduly contracted and hurried.

The Western comic book has traveled the same route in reverse—from simplicity of detail in such early features as *Tom Mix* and *Roy Rogers* to the elaborateness of *Red Wolf* and *Jonah Hex*. In *Red Wolf* especially the land was integrated into the main motivation of the hero. It was from the land and the generations of warriors who had personified it that the hero drew his strength and his justification, in the manner of a modern Anteus.

The Garden of the West, however, has always been more than mere rock and water. The vegetation, the flora of the West have become familiar landmarks to every reader of the comics: the ever-present cactus, whose motif serves as a kind of shorthand (its use could be subtly allegorical, as in *Krazy Kat* or *Little Jimmy*, or routinely descriptive as in *The Lone Ranger*); and the meagre mesquite are the most common. But there are also the towering pine forests of *King of the Mounties*, the lonely sagamores of *Red Ryder*, the hospitable and shady groves of *The Cisco Kid*. Wild prairie flowers often form a multi-colored tapestry in the more inspired Sunday pages of *Rick O'Shay*.

The seasons also play a great role in the Western comics: the scorching desert sun under which Red Ryder or Blueberry unrelentingly pursue their quarry, the blizzards that hamper Sergeant King's fateful errands, the dust storms that throw Hopalong Cassidy or Kid Colt off the trail, are but one more variable in the unpredictable mood of the West.

Animals form a part of Nature's bounty in the Garden of the West. King or Red Ryder have often feasted on venison or on the meat of the jackrabbit, while salmon swimming upstream have been the salvation of many a traveler or prospector lost in some mountain wilderness. Hunting and fishing scenes have long been a staple of Western comics. They were most realistic in J. R. Williams's *Out Our Way*, most bucolic in *Little Jimmy*, most dramatic in *Casey Ruggles*. More than any other theme they set the Western apart from all other action-oriented strips. Not that hunting and fishing are uncommon in other adventure comics (they abound in *Tarzan* and *Jungle Jim*, to cite only two instances), but in the context of the West they acquire a more immediate meaning, absent from the more exotic goings-on of the jungle strips.

The Garden of the West, the reader is often reminded, is not a peaceable kingdom. The Western heroes often had to fight wolves, grizzly bears, mountain lions and wild bulls in a kind of primitive duel in

Allen Dean, *King of the Royal Mounted*. The characters are dwarfed by the majesty of the land. © King Features Syndicate.

Gir, *Lieutenant Blueberry*. The land plays a major part in the action. © Editions Dargaud.

which the man is only armed with a knife or a lariat to protect him against the teeth and claws of the wild beasts. Such vagaries of the man vs. beast theme as the giant insects in *Tomahawk*, the supernatural wolf in *Red Wolf*, or the horse-mounted gorillas in *Tex Willer* also deserve passing mention.

Finally there is the permanent mark of man's passage writ large on the face of the land. Human settlements may be only dots on the map, but they acquire ominous significance in that they are not born of the land, but set against it. An abnormal excrescence, they provide the necessary conflict that endows life in the West with its unique meaning: the ultimate confrontation between man and nature.

Gardner Fox and Syd Shores, *Red Wolf*. It was from the land and the generations of warriors who had personified it that the hero drew his strength. © Marvel Comics Group.

Jack King, *The Gun That Won the West*. The Garden of the West is not always a peaceable kingdom. © Olin Corporation.

Every conceivable form of human settlement has been depicted in the comics of the American West, from the primitive huts of lonely fur trappers to the sinful splendors of Denver and San Francisco, but the frontier town has proved a perennial favorite of comic strip artists. Patterned on the model of Tombstone or Dodge City during its heyday, it allows for almost perfect perspective along the axis of its main street. It also gives cartoonists an opportunity to show off their virtuosity in the lusty depiction of gambling dens and drinking saloons, and the colorful rendering of ramshackle houses and establishments of commerce.

In the course of their careers each cartoonist seems to have developed his own specialty. Lonely cavalry outposts are Gir's *forte* in *Lieutenant Blueberry;* Fred Harman shows a marked predilection for Indian cliff-dwellings in *Bronc Peeler*, and for ghost towns in *Red Ryder;* opulent if incongruous settings are the hallmark of *Lance;* mining towns are a recurring motif in *Randall;* and outlaw hideaways speck the landscape in *The Rawhide Kid.*

Whatever their divergent characteristics, these testimonials to man's unceasing activity and unmitigated endurance symbolize one thread that runs all through the history of the West: the despoiling of a once virgin land.

The people

Life on the frontier never was easy. Out of the hardships arising from the constant struggle against a recalcitrant soil, hostile elements, and bellicose native tribes there emerged a new breed of men, tough, suspicious, rugged, and heroic. Whether, as some have contended (chief among them John Wayne who has made a career of impersonating just such a man), the Westerner was a special being, or whether, as is commonly argued, he was only an ordinary mortal pit-

Fred Ray and Ed Herron, *Tomahawk*. Man vs. giant insects, in one of the weirder sequences of the Western saga. © DC Comics, Inc.

ted against extraordinary circumstances, is not at issue. What concerns us here is not the sociological truth, but the aesthetic truth, deeper and more revealing.

The first white men to penetrate the Western wilderness were trappers, hunters and mountain men. They were often first also in opening new trails and mapping out the new country. Yet few of their numbers found their way into the comic pages, perhaps because cartoonists were less concerned with the era of slow penetration than with the more colorful period of heady conquest and spectacular consolidation.

The only mountain man to be featured as the hero of a comic strip, for instance, is Buddy Longway, and the feature appears to be far less successful than Greg's more conventional *Comanche*.

Trappers have played a greater role in the comics. Fur trappers have been one of the mainstays of *King of the Mounties*, and they have also figured prominently in *Casey Ruggles*. Jim Boum has often been engaged in trapping and hunting activities, and these have formed the schemes of some of his most memorable adventures.

Giovanni Ticci, *Tex Willer*. A typical Western town as depicted in the comics. © Edizioni Araldo.

Gold prospecting, on the other hand, is an activity often depicted in the comics. As we have seen in an earlier chapter, the lure of gold is what attracted such comic figures as Mickey Mouse and Popeye to the Western wilderness. Gold has also provided many Western scriptwriters with one of the prime human motivations—greed—which leads to violent conflict. *Red Ryder*, *The Lone Ranger*, *Little Joe*, *Kit Carson*, there is practically no Western feature that hasn't utilized this ready-made device.

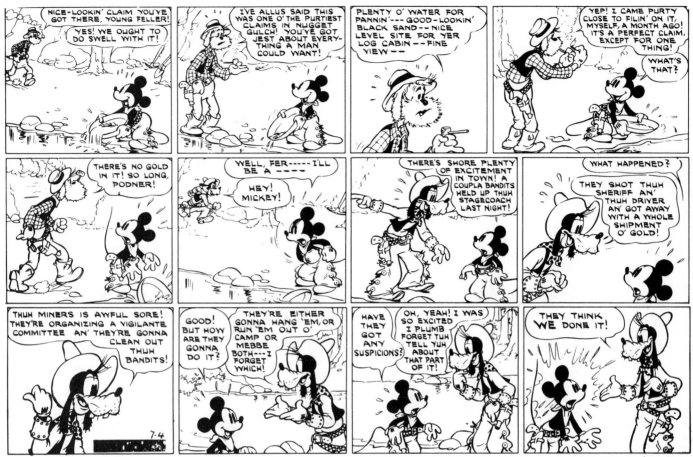

Floyd Gottfredson, *Mickey Mouse*. Panning for gold with Mickey and Goofy. © Walt Disney Productions.

The Westerner most often seen in comic strips and comic books, as well as in the movies, is the ubiquitous cowboy. Somehow sheepmen hardly ever managed to get anybody's attention except as foils. The cowboys, in reality as in legend, were a boisterous, hard-driving, hard-fighting, unshaven and colorful lot. No cartoonist quite captured their independent and querulous spirit as did J. R. Williams in *Out Our Way*. The noted Western authority J. Frank Dobie once wrote admiringly to the artist: "Man, you've got something that beats cleverness all hollow. You've got humanity and the power of seeing things and the ability to translate concrete observation and humanity into lines."

The un-idealized (or little idealized) figure of the cowboy also came forcefully through in the drawings of Fred Harman; not so much with Red Ryder who had already undergone the fateful transformation into hero as in such secondary characters as Coyote Pete, Red's ranching friend Randy, and even the redoubtable Duchess. And of course Harman's didactic features (*On the Range, Cowboys*, etc.) were loving dedications to the works, joys and hardships of the range riders.

Two comic features that are notable for their minute descriptions of ranch life, separated by a chasm of over 30 years, as well as by the width of an ocean are

Fred Harman, *Red Ryder*. The cowboy as quintessential hero of the West. © Hawley Publications.

Al Carreño's *Ted Strong* (at least in its first period) and Greg and Hermann's *Comanche*. They have both used authentic and well-documented Western locales as realistic backdrops to the imaginary exploits of their respective heroes.

Only slightly larger than life the figure of Utah dominated the action of *Little Joe*. The aging, gruff cowhand whose eye is still sharp and whose grip still deadly is of course a mainstay of Western lore. As depicted by Leffingwell he cut a disquieting figure, midway between that of fairy-tale savior and dime-novel rogue.

In modern times Stan Lynde has in the main remained faithful to authentic details, customs and mannerisms typical of the West, in his strip, *Rick O'Shay*. His hero, however, while still displaying on occasion stature and pathos, is already a long stride away from the historical West, and is traveling ever outwards in the direction of the lunatic reaches of *Tumbleweeds*, where epic has given way to parody, and the cowboy is depicted as a clown on horseback.

All the familiar figures of the American West: the blacksmith, the sheep herder, the saloon keeper, the schoolmarm, not to mention the undertaker, have appeared prominently in the comics. Their roles were usually played in the background, where they could serve as a kind of Greek chorus, in counterpoint to the fateful goings-on taking place on stage center.

Next to the cowboys, the U.S. Army, and especially the Cavalry, has long been a favorite of the cartoonists. Actually only Warren Tuft's *Lance* had the main action centered around army life and military feats of valor (this in contrast to film Westerns that often had military men as their protagonists, notably in the movies of John Ford). The reason for this paucity of military heroes in the comics is simple: the strictures of military life are inimical to the requirements of the comic hero who, above all else, must remain free and unfettered. In the comics the Army was most often seen as a homogeneous, coherent body, from which few protagonists of singular stature emerged. Rather than the embodiment of a myth it was the reassuring symbol of a faraway authority, the Great White Father in Washington.

On the other hand, para-military outfits were not so constrained (at least in the eyes of scriptwriters) and accordingly Canadian Mounties and Texas Rangers were especially popular protagonists in the comics. They combined rugged individuality (as they went about their assignments on their own) with the prestige of a dashing uniform and a time-honored aura of bravery and determination ("a Mountie always gets his man.") The same formula was also applied to Army scouts who were shown as romantic outriders in such features as *Jed Cooper* or *Old Scout*.

In recent times there has been a tendency (especially marked in Europe) towards a revisionist version of the role played by the U.S. Army in the West. Lieutenant Blueberry is often seen at odds with the policies of his superiors, and *Sgt. Kirk* had an army deserter as its hero. In the United States it has become fashionable to depict the soldiers of the West as blundering fools rather than bloodthirsty villains. The trend is most glaringly exposed in the recently created *Catfish*.

The Indians are, of course, America's first inhabitants, and the way they have been pictured in the comics is worthy of notice. By and large it is fair to say that the red man has always gotten a better deal in the comics than in the movies. While it is true that the Indians have sometimes been portrayed as murdering savages (and even compared to vermin in *Jed Cooper*), they were even more often depicted with warmth and sympathy for their plight, and understanding for their customs, as in *Little Jimmy*; in *White Boy* the red man's way of life came through clearly as being superior to that of the white people. This sympathetic view of the Indian is best exemplified in this quote taken from Fred Harman at his folksiest (in *On the Range*): "History books tell us about wild Injuns and how they killed white people. When they weren't killin' cowboys an' soldiers, they were fightin' other Injun tribes. But schucks, ya can't blame them fer all the massacres. They were pikers compared to us folks."

The Indian sidekick was a staple of the medium: the Lone Ranger had Tonto, and Red Ryder Little Beaver, to cite the two most prominent cases; and while the custom is now seen as being patronizing it certainly was not perceived in that light by the artists. Tonto displayed a bravery and heroism that most white people proved themselves incapable of, and Little Beaver showed more courage, initiative, acumen and resourcefulness than any of his white companions or schoolmates.

James Swinnerton, *Little Jimmy*. The Indians were portrayed with warmth and sympathy in this Swinnerton creation. © King Features Syndicate.

It is true, however, that the comics took a long time before they featured an Indian in the title role. There have been *Straight Arrow*, *Strong Bow* and, closer to us, *Red Wolf*. European cartoonists have been bolder, with *Winnetou* in Germany, and especially with the fascinating *De Indianen* series in the Netherlands. How far the red man has come in the comics can best be seen, however, in an American feature, *Redeye*, which does to the legend of nature's nobleman what *Tumbleweeds* does to the myth of the Western hero. In terms of parody and satire at least, Indian and cowboy are now treated with admirable if back-handed equality.

John Belfi, *Straight Arrow*. Straight Arrow was one of the few Indian heroes of Western comics. © Bell Syndicate.

The legend

There is something in the vastness of the American continent and the awesomeness of the Western sky that lends itself to myth-making. The Indians created cosmogonical legends and the cowboys came up with the tall tale. As with ancient Greece the historians have always found it difficult to sort out fact from fiction, to find when history began and legend ended. Everything that touches the West has been transmogrified into allegory and symbol, and it is precisely that metamorphosis that makes any study of the West in history or fiction so fascinating. It is a return to the fount of human imagination.

The legend of the West started even before the War of Independence. It received an added impetus from the French and Indian Wars, and reached the public consciousness with the Louisiana Purchase and the Merriwether-Clark expedition. This period of American history, while not widely reflected in the comics, did not go unnoticed with the several comic books devoted to Daniel Boone embellishing on the accounts of the famed frontier fighter's exploits. Such non-Western strips as *Dick's Adventures in Dreamland*, in which the twelve-year old title character dreamed his way through American history, and *Dickie Dare*, also recalled the period in some of their episodes.

The period of expansion and the war with Mexico was probably even better documented (or embroidered upon) with the Davy Crockett craze of the mid-Fifties. "Remember the Alamo!" became a renewed battle cry as cartoonists all over the world rushed pell-mell to celebrate the heroic defenders of the Texas fort. The embrace even extended to lesser figures such as Jim Bowie who enjoyed his own comic book for a brief time.

The comics, like the movies, lavished most of their attention, however, to the era of massive white settlement of the West that followed the Civil War. The most visible symbol of the trek westward was the wagon train, and cartoonists never seemed to tire of depicting the long convoys of covered wagons slowly winding their way through the dusty plains, arid deserts and lofty mountain passes of the West.

Antonio Canale and Sergio Tuis, *Kirbi Flint*. The wagon train: one of the most enduring clichés of the Western scene. © Editrice L.P.

LA VALLE DEGLI UOMINI PERDUTI

QUELLA MATTINA KIRBI FLINT, IL FAMOSO SCOUT AL SERVIZIO DEL GOVERNO, SI E' RIDESTATO UN POCO TRISTE. UN PENSIERO E' RITORNATO NELLA SUA MENTE ED HA CANCELLATO DAL SUO VOLTO LA CONSUETA ESPRESSIONE ALLEGRA. AFFACCIANDOSI ALLA FINESTRA . . .

DA QUALCHE TEMPO TUTTO MARCIA BENE NEL PAESE E NEI DINTORNI... SEMBRA CHE BANDITI E PREPOTENTI DI OGNI SPECIE SIANO SCOMPARSI PER SEMPRE, MA NON C'E' DA FARSI ILLUSIONI!...

5-1

The first Sunday episode of *The Lone Ranger* newspaper strip was centered around the intended ambush of wagon train travelers (foiled in the nick of time by the masked hero, naturally). There were similar episodes in *Bronco Bill*, *Death Valley* and *Matt Mariott*, among the many strips that used the theme. There was even the short-lived *Wagon Train* comic book (based on the TV series) published by Dell in the Sixties.

In continental Europe the theme was picked up by Morris and Goscinny in *Lucky Luke*, most memorably in an episode titled "The Caravan," and provided Greg and Derib with the main plot of the semihumorous *Go West!* in the Seventies.

Harry O'Neill, *Bronco Bill*. This convoy is headed for a long and suspenseful journey, as any reader of Western comics can easily imagine. © United Feature Syndicate.

Another true-life Western intiative that was later magnified into a legend was the Pony Express. Actually this experiment in fast mail service lasted for only 18 months in 1860 and 1861, but the daredevil Pony Express riders so captured the public imagination that in this short time they had become living legends. The exploits of the more fabled of them found their way into the countless *Buffalo Bill* comic strip and comic book versions published here and abroad (notably *Cody of the Pony Express* whose focus was on precisely that short period in Western history), and in the *Wild Bill Hickok* comic books although Hickok himself had not been a rider, contrary to legend, but a station hand.

The conquest of the West was, in no small part, a triumph of transportation, of brave and resourceful stagecoach drivers defying the perils of momentous journeys that included dust storms, blizzards, Indian raiders, and road agents. In his moments of temporary impecuniousness Red Ryder, for one, was not adverse to riding shotgun on a coach for a fee, and the first episode of *Comanche* involved a long and eventful coach ride.

After the stagecoach there came the railroad, and the exhilarating accounts of the building of the first transcontinental railway found echoes in many a comic strip. Perhaps the most dramatic recreation of this saga came in a long episode of *Lieutenant Blueberry*, which bore (not coincidentally) the same title as that of John Ford's silent classic, *The Iron Horse*. The sequence in which the train engineer and Blueberry, trying to escape from a raiding party of Indians under the leadership of Red Cloud, drive the machine across a flaming bridge, is worthy of an almost similar incident in Cecil B. DeMille's *Union Pacific* which obviously inspired it.

The multiplication of stagecoach lines and the greater reliability of railroad schedules inevitably brought with them an increased frequency of Indian attacks and armed holdups. Here we have another instance of real-life occurrences blown up to the proportions of legend. Such incidents were proportionately no more frequent than muggings in New York City, but lurid newspaper accounts, fawning on such figures as the James brothers and Geronimo, have permanently established the almost fatal inevitability of such attacks in the public mind: was there ever a train or a stagecoach in movie or comic strip that enjoyed a peaceful journey? American desperadoes and Mexican bandidos regularly attacked stagecoaches in *Red Ryder*, Apache renegades ambushed these same stagecoaches as a matter of routine in *The Cisco Kid*, and blowing up trains for whatever purpose was a favorite pastime of outlaws in *The Lone Ranger*. In the comics railway and coach lines, it would seem at times, were run solely in order to provide the hero with a sure-fire way of proving his prowess.

"Gold! gold in the American River!" This fateful cry sparked yet another legendary incident of Western history: the famous Gold Rush of 1849, whose overtones and undertones have haunted our collective memory for more than a century. *Casey Ruggles* is the

Rod Reed and José-Luis Salinas, *The Cisco Kid*. The classic stagecoach holdup. © King Features Syndicate.

Warren Tufts, *Casey Ruggles*. Greed and lust in the Old West. © United Feature Syndicate.

only American strip that directly dealt with the implications of the discovery of gold at Sutter's Mill. Warren Tufts depicted with unadorned, sometimes even grim, authenticity the changes visited by greed and lust upon an idyllic countryside. The theme was also explored in such features as *Hopalong Cassidy*, where it was lightly disposed of. Only Hernandez Palacios in *Manos Kelly* has been able to match Tufts in the historical recreation of a colorful but lawless, and sometimes squalid, episode of the Western odyssey.

Even more firmly implanted in the public perception of the West is the elaborate folklore that surrounds accounts of cowboy life on the range. The cattle drives are especially singled out, both as genuine testimony to the cowboy's toughness and endurance and as moral allegory of man's ultimate triumph over the blind forces of nature. To Western strip artists the cattle drives provided all the elements of a true-life epic: suspense, action, cliff-hanging, tension, conflict, as well as a splendid imagery of cattle stampedes, desert treks, night rides and gun battles. *Red Ryder* and *Wild Bill Pecos* immediately come to mind as two features that made extensive use of the device; and the theme also provided one of the few gripping episodes of *Broncho Bill,* in which Bill and his Rangers drove several thousand head of cattle across the treacherous waters of the Missouri.

Another instance where Western history has come down to us in the form of cowboy legend is provided by the not uncommon range wars that pitted rival cattlemen against one another. This theme forms the almost exclusive plotline of *Tex Thorne*, in which competing ranch owners engaged in bloody and obscurely motivated feuds, with the enigmatic Tex holding the balance of power which he chose to shift according to his own ambiguous moral code. This constant tug-of-war gave to the feature an unsettling quality that probably proved its undoing.

No single Western episode has enjoyed such mythi-

Zane Grey and Allen Dean, *Tex Thorne.*
Another staple of the Western genre: the
cattle drive. © King Features Syndicate.

cal exemplariness as the bloody encounter at the O.K. Corral. This incident gave rise to the by now well-entrenched convention of the showdown at high noon, the high point in any Western saga worth its salt. The gunfight itself has been recounted innumerable times in comic books (*Wyatt Earp, Tombstone Territory,* etc.) but, beyond the real-life happening, the dramatic device of the shootout "fair and square" has become a hallmark of the comics, especially in traditional Westerns such as *Hopalong Cassidy* and *Tom Mix* in the United States, *Tex Willer, Gun Law* and *Randall* in Europe and South America.

In order to settle the land the Westerners had to displace the first inhabitants, the Indians. The fact could not be ignored, although it could be glossed over as it was in most comic features. Those features that chose to tackle the Indian problem head-on usually came down on the side of traditional Western history. Thus the French version of *Buffalo Bill* recounted in profuse detail the totally fictitious duel between the Army scout and the Indian chief Yellow Hand; while the Italian *Kit Carson* turned Sitting Bull's daring raid on Fort Rice in 1865 into a U.S. victory. The causes as well as the savagery (on both sides) of the Indian wars were more objectively reported by Warren Tufts in *Lance,* while Hans G. Kresse is currently giving his readers a highly romanticized account of the struggle, as seen from the Indian side, in *De Indianen.*

With the end of the Indian wars civilization came to the West. Such amenities as the galvanized bathtub (immortalized by J. R. Williams in *Out Our Way*), the coal stove and the paved sidewalk made their appearance, to the initial bemusement of the local

Aurelio Galleppini, *Tex Willer.* Cowboys vs. Indians. © Edizioni Araldo.

citizenry. The opening of schools and the general introduction of compulsory education brought about the familiar figure of the schoolmarm, usually portrayed in the comics as attractive and suitably demure—a staple of the genre in such features as *The Cisco Kid* and *Red Ryder*, in which the hero could often be seen vying for the favors of the damsel, in direct competition to the evil designs of snarling and bemoustached villains. While school was suitable for the usual run of cow town kids, it only incited such stalwarts as Little Beaver or Broncho Bill's companions into playing hooky (usually to their chagrin).

All the tales that came to make up the collective folklore of the West have, at one time or another, found their way into the comics. Hernando de Soto's

V. Chiomenti, *Davy Crockett*. The legendary Alamo defender has now become a worldwide figure of Western mythology. © Edizioni Alpe.

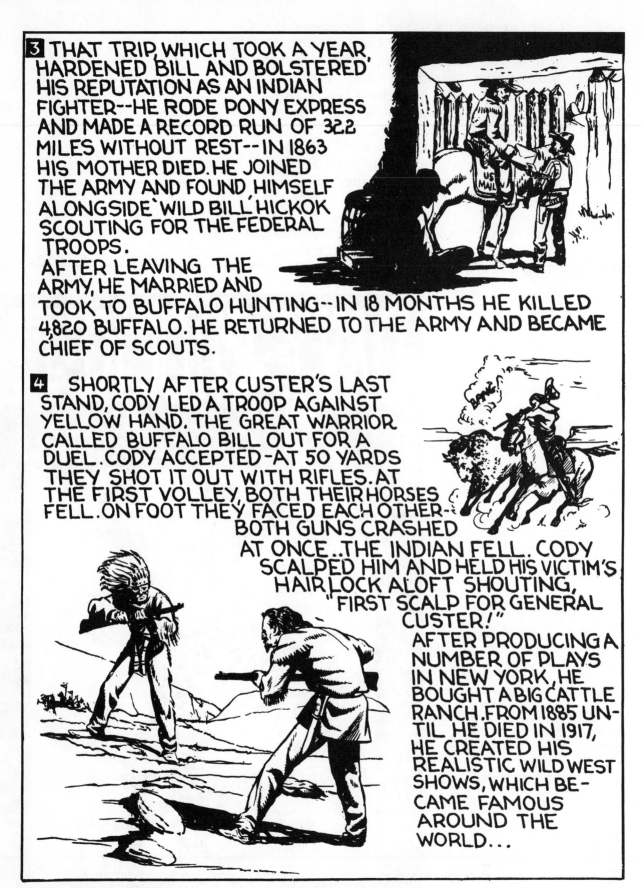

3 THAT TRIP, WHICH TOOK A YEAR, HARDENED BILL AND BOLSTERED HIS REPUTATION AS AN INDIAN FIGHTER--HE RODE PONY EXPRESS AND MADE A RECORD RUN OF 322 MILES WITHOUT REST--IN 1863 HIS MOTHER DIED. HE JOINED THE ARMY AND FOUND HIMSELF ALONGSIDE WILD BILL HICKOK SCOUTING FOR THE FEDERAL TROOPS.
AFTER LEAVING THE ARMY, HE MARRIED AND TOOK TO BUFFALO HUNTING--IN 18 MONTHS HE KILLED 4,820 BUFFALO. HE RETURNED TO THE ARMY AND BECAME CHIEF OF SCOUTS.

4 SHORTLY AFTER CUSTER'S LAST STAND, CODY LED A TROOP AGAINST YELLOW HAND. THE GREAT WARRIOR CALLED BUFFALO BILL OUT FOR A DUEL. CODY ACCEPTED -AT 50 YARDS THEY SHOT IT OUT WITH RIFLES. AT THE FIRST VOLLEY, BOTH THEIR HORSES FELL. ON FOOT THEY FACED EACH OTHER-- BOTH GUNS CRASHED AT ONCE..THE INDIAN FELL. CODY SCALPED HIM AND HELD HIS VICTIM'S HAIR LOCK ALOFT SHOUTING, "FIRST SCALP FOR GENERAL CUSTER!"
AFTER PRODUCING A NUMBER OF PLAYS IN NEW YORK, HE BOUGHT A BIG CATTLE RANCH. FROM 1885 UN- TIL HE DIED IN 1917, HE CREATED HIS REALISTIC WILD WEST SHOWS, WHICH BE- CAME FAMOUS AROUND THE WORLD...

Will Eisner, *Buffalo Bill*. This graphic depiction of Colonel Cody's legendary exploits was one of Will Eisner's first comic book assignments. © S.M. Iger.

fruitless search for the Seven Cities of Cibola have found their counterpart in Bronc Peeler's or Red Ryder's discoveries of lost Indian civilizations, direct descendants of the fabled Cibolans; while the legend of the Lost Dutchman's Mine has been the subject of a highly original and dramatic interpretation in *Lieutenant Blueberry*.

Stan Lynde, *Rick O'Shay*. Famed marshal Wild Bill Hickok making a cameo appearance in *Rick O'Shay*. © Chicago Tribune-New York News Syndicate.

A legend, any legend, needs larger-than-life figures to sustain and perpetuate it. Greek mythology had Achilles and Ulysses and Ajax and Theseus; Western mythology has Buffalo Bill and Davy Crockett, Kit Carson and Billy the Kid. If numbers are any guide, Buffalo Bill is the Western figure most often mythified in the United States as well as abroad. There seems to be no country that does not have at least one version of the life and times of the Western scout, a phenomenon perhaps more revealing of Colonel Cody's uncanny ability as a showman than of his exploits as a guide and Indian fighter.

With the exception of Albertarelli's and Molino's remarkable *Kit Carson*, historical figures have given birth to a disappointingly low number of correspondingly worthwhile features. Of the hundreds of *Buffalo Bill* versions that have afflicted the comic pages from one end of the earth to the other, there aren't more than two or three that are even remotely commendable. The many *Davy Crockett* and *Daniel Boone* comic books are best left forgotten, and the same holds sadly true for all the *Wild Bill Hickok, Calamity Jane, Jim Bowie* and *Annie Oakley* comics that have seen the light of print here and abroad.

Yet these hero-worshipping features will keep coming, as long as the myth of the West is kept alive in the breast of modern man. In spite of all the exposés and debunkings (of which the movie *Buffalo Bill and the Indians* is the most recent example), our adulation for the legendary heroes of the West will never die, for modern man needs the comfort of a myth more than ever. Upon learning that the Tom Mix legend was a hoax perpetrated by clever press agents, popular historian Jim Harmon was moved to write (in his *Nostalgia Catalogue*):

"Personally, I prefer to recall the story in my Ralston Straight Shooters Manual, with its "Tom Mix Chart of Wounds" showing twelve bullet wounds and forty-seven bone fractures (not shown were twenty-two knife wounds or the four-inch hole in his back caused by a dynamite explosion). The story in the manual may not have been the truth, but it was better than the truth—it was adventure, excitement, impossible idealism. Now that I know the true story, I shall certainly do my best to forget it."

Harry Bishop, *Gun Law*. Marshal Matt Dillon in the role created on TV by James Arness. © Daily Express.

The same adulation and idealization have surrounded some Western cartoonists. As Fred Harman was to admit candidly in an interview given to the magazine *True West*: "Much has been written about me as the creator of the comic strip *Red Ryder* and Little Beaver. Some of it was true but in some cases my part as the "living" Red Ryder in a rodeo arena was blown higher than a kite to please millions of young hero-worshipping fans."

Feeding incessantly upon itself, piling fictitious details upon real incidents, and pious fabulation upon historical truth, the legend unalterably lives on.

The hero

As a living and organic body of myths, the Western legend found its ideal incarnation in the Western hero. As has been seen in an earlier paragraph historical figures were elevated to the status of demigods, but the process was to be enlarged further, building not on the concrete precedent of flesh-and-blood mortals out of the living past, but on the construction of fictional figures from abstract archetypes.

Carlos Freixas, *Pistol Jim*. The archetypal cowboy-hero is an internationally recognized symbol of justice. © Carlos Freixas.

The first archetype to emerge clearly from Western history and folklore was that of The Lawman, born from such fabulous incidents as the gunfight at O.K. Corral, the cleaning up of Tombstone, and the Lincoln County range wars. Local sheriffs and United States marshals acquired an aura of righteousness and invincibility often far removed from documented facts.

It is interesting to note, however, that few American comic features have had a lawman as their titular hero. There was the short-lived *Rocky Mason, Government Marshal* in the newspapers, and *Wyatt Earp* and *Sheriff of Tombstone* in comic books, and that's about all. The record is not much better overseas with only *Gun Law* (which has Marshal Matt Dillon as the hero) in England, *Tex Willer* (a Texas Ranger) and *Il Piccolo/Nuovo Sceriffo* in Italy to uphold the genre. (*Rick O'Shay* is a special case in that his authority derived at first from a rather dubious source.)

What probably accounts for this paradoxical fact is the organic structure of the comics: unlike a film, which is structurally self-contained, no matter how many titles there may be in a given series, a comic feature is open-ended, and does not easily accommodate itself to hierarchical order. In the comics the most popular heroes have always been the freebooters, and authority, no matter how far removed or ineffective, gets in the way of comic strip story-telling after a number of years. That is why Tex Willer or Matt Dillon so often stray from their official duties to run into wild adventures in which the rules no longer apply.

Even the inclusion of Canadian Mountie strips (*King of the Royal Mounted, Men of the Mounted,* etc.) does not appreciably improve this disappointing performance on the part of the lawmen. Clearly the comics were in need of some other archetype than The Lawman, from which they could derive little.

The archetype upon which the comics have been chiefly relying is that of The Cowboy. Unlike the lawman the cowboy has no official standing, but he is distinguished by a recognizable aura of righteousness (as well as by a fast draw), and his sanction comes from the respect and admiration of his fellow citizens. To assuage the fears of some that he may turn into a vigilante, the cowboy was given a set of reassuring values that found their most popularly accepted expression in Gene Autry's famous "Ten Commandments of the Cowboy." George Fenin and William Everson, in their excellent study *The Western,* have put it succinctly:

"He [the cowboy] must not take unfair advantage, even when facing an enemy. He must never go back on his word, or on the trust confided in him. He must always tell the truth, be gentle with children, elderly people, and animals. He must not advocate or possess racially or religiously intolerant ideas. Moreover, he must help people in distress, be a good worker, keep himself clean in thought, speech, action, and personal habits. He must respect women, parents, and his nation's laws. He must neither drink nor smoke. And finally, the cowboy is a patriot."

This whitewashed version of the cowboy archetype was adopted by a number of newspaper strips and comic books, notably those based on Western movie heroes. Thus both *Gene Autry Rides!* and the *Gene*

Autry comic books ran true to type, as could be expected; and so did *Tom Mix, Roy Rogers* and *Buck Jones.* The classic example of the cowboy as a pillar of rectitude was best provided, however, by Hopalong Cassidy who, in spite of his black outfit, could have easily passed for a Western version of Mr. Clean. Fred Harman's creations diverge somewhat from the norm (*Bronc Peeler* in its whimsicality, *Red Ryder* in its earthiness and skepticism), but his heroes are nonetheless formed from the same mold.

Abroad the type has inspired numerous incarnations, the most egregious being *Jim Boum, Pistol Jim* and *The Lone Star Rider*. It should also be noted that, despite their sometimes self-deprecating humor, the heroes of *Rick O'Shay* and *Lucky Luke* belong absolutely to this tradition, and that the elements of parody present in these two strips are aimed at the conventions and stereotypes of the Western, and not at the genre's moral implications. The same does not hold true in the iconoclastic *Cocco Bill* and *Tumbleweeds*, in which all the accepted assumptions and traditional values of the genre are joyously demolished.

Frank Bellamy, *Swade*. The lone rider of the Plains. © Frank Bellamy.

In opposition to what may be called the ethically conscious cowboy there stands The Lone Rider who knows no code other than his own. Unlike the earlier archetype he seeks no outside recognition or sanction, but is driven by an inner conviction or by personal motivations. More than any other author Zane Grey has made this kind of lonely hero his own; it is therefore no surprise to discover that the comic feature most representative of the type should be the Grey-inspired *Tex Thorne*. The hard edge and pessimism implicit in such a hero did not go down well with American comic strip readers, however; and the genre has not been markedly popular in the United States. On the other hand it was enthusiastically seized upon in other countries, and put to remarkable and dramatic use by such as the Belgian Jijé in *Jerry Spring*, the Argentinian Del Castillo in *Randall*, and the Mexican Suarez Lozano in *Alma Grande*. Under the skillful pen of these artists the heroes have become the modern counterparts of the knights errant.

A more established type of Western hero has been the lovable rogue, whose inspiration is also medieval, going back to Robin Hood. Both *The Cisco Kid* and *Maverick* are good examples of the genre, in which the protagonist makes up for his (usually trivial) peccadilloes by a show of bravery and selflessness. Thus it is not unusual to see the seemingly tough-minded Bret Maverick give up an easy mark at a poker game for the far less lucrative and also far more perilous task of helping an old rancher get his farm back from the hands of unscrupulous operators.

Proceeding one step further we now come across that familiar figure, the reformed outlaw. The reformed outlaw is always pursued by the blind forces of society for his past trespasses, whether those are contrived (the hero has been framed for somebody else's crime, as in *Lieutenant Blueberry*), or real but

Nicholas Cardy and Mike Sekowsky, *Bat Lash*. The reformed outlaw is a familiar figure of Western mythology. © DC Comics, Inc.

Charles Flanders, *The Lone Ranger*. The masked Western hero has by now become a staple of the genre. © King Features Syndicate.

excusable (the hero had to kill in self-defense, as in *Kid Colt*). The genre of course is as old as Victor Hugo's *Les Misérables*, but its built-in conflict never ceases to grip the audience. Perhaps more stylistically interesting is the variation on the same theme provided by Jonah Hex. In this case the hero's conflict is all interior, as we witness his being torn between heroism and villainy (or at least callousness.) Heroism, however, always wins the day in the end.

All these variations on the original archetype (based on the bad guy/hero antinomy derived from romantic and later popular literature) provide the Western author with an additional element of suspense (and of ambiguity): that of the pursuer suddenly turned fugitive, or of the upholder of the law having to flee the legal authorities. In the hands of a master story-teller this could be the most gripping element of all but, unfortunately, Western comic writers have only used the situation in the most superficial and sophomoric way (such as having a bank robber recognize Kid Colt and try to pin his crime on him, or some suspicious sheriff break up the Cisco Kid's flirtation with some attractive damsel he just happened to have rescued.)

The masked Western hero also derives from literary precedent (in this instance the *Zorro* novels). In the comics *The Lone Ranger* was undoubtedly the first protagonist to wear a mask, a convention not conspicuously picked up by other newspaper strips. It is an altogether different matter in the comic books where the trend towards masked and, when at all possible, costumed Western heroes has been overwhelming from the start. There have been Durango Kid, the Outlaw Kid, the Masked Raider, Nighthawk, the Ghost Rider, and countless others who have donned mask or disguise for the most arbitrary (and often the most laughable) of reasons. The real motiva-

Stan Lee and Doug Wildey, *Man With a Gun.* The Western tale is the modern equivalent of the medieval morality play. © Marvel Comics Group.

tion, of course, has always been crassly commercial: to try and relate the Western tradition to the vastly more popular (to the comic book audience) concept of the super-hero. Only in *Red Wolf* was an intelligent attempt made at organically incorporating elements of the super-hero ethos into the Western mythos; because of its very sophisticated and intricate weaving together of two distinct traditions, the experiment unfortunately failed, and it is not likely to be tried again in the foreseeable future.

The Cowboy, like all archetypes, could easily be recognized by exterior and unmistakable clues. There was his costume, of course, that differed in some small but telling detail from that of the other characters around him (Red Ryder's red shirt, Hopalong Cassidy's black outfit, the Rawhide Kid's square-rigged Stetson). There was also his manner, neither arrogant nor self-assuming (as that of the villain), nor submissive or meek (as that of the victims). Clearly there was a free man, walking tall, standing straight, and riding high.

But (and this was the clincher), above all things, there was the cowboy's horse. The hero's stallion (not necessarily white, as legend falsely has it) was nonetheless no ordinary mount, but the equine replica of his master, a prince among beasts just as the hero was a prince among men. No cowboy was without his four-legged companion in circumstances fair and foul, his friend of all seasons, and sometimes his rescuer of last resort. Tom Mix had Tony, Red Ryder had Thunder, the Lone Ranger had Silver, and so on *ad infinitum*. All these, and countless others (Scout, Lightning, Trigger, Blackie, in a wild array of palominos and pintos, Arabians and mustangs) displayed qualities whose aggregate would be impossible in humans: they had intelligence, loyalty, cleverness, endurance, compassion, not to mention fleet-footedness and incredible stamina. In the West, at least, man's best friend was not his dog; and the instances of a Western horse saving his master's life are legion in the literature of the genre. In Western legend man and horse were but one: the triumphant reincarnation of the mythical centaur of old.

The antagonist

If the hero was the upholder of law and justice in the territories of the West, the bad man, outlaw or desperado was perceived not just as a menace to the social order, but as a direct challenge to the moral authority of the hero. He was the negative side of all the values that the hero embodied. This is nowhere as evident as in those comic strip sequences in which the townspeople (or ranchers, or miners, as the case may

© 1975 by The Chicago Tribune
All Rights Reserved

Stan Lynde, *Rick O'Shay*. It is the villain who triggers the action in Western comics. © Chicago Tribune-New York News Syndicate.

be) turn against the hero under the clever proddings or the outright blandishments of scheming villains. In a 1940 *Red Ryder* episode, for instance, Red had to fight off a lynch mob bent on hanging an innocent farmer framed for murder. Similar incidents can also be found in *The Lone Ranger*, *King of the Mounties*, *The Rawhide Kid*, *Rick O'Shay*, or any number of comic strip Westerns. In the end, of course, the hero manages to rally the misguided people to the cause of justice, and the real criminal is unmasked, often through a stratagem devised to secure a self-confession. Perhaps the villain will gloat of his crime to the tied-up hero, as in *Red Ryder*, unaware that the sheriff and his deputies, alerted by Little Beaver, are listening behind the door.

That the populace can be so easily swayed or deceived directly points to the necessity of having a hero whose morals are exemplary; it also raises the villain above the trivial motivations of his deeds—greed, gold lust, envy, thirst for revenge—and thrusts him into the role of antagonist or anti-hero. His mission, whether he himself realizes it or not, is to oppose the hero in black and white terms that can be immediately understood by all. Thus we are witnessing a morality play in which the Protagonist and the Antagonist are locked in mortal (and moral) combat. A Western is not all that removed from *Paradise Lost*, and each of its episodes can be said to roughly correspond to a song in an epic poem. As the representative of changeless order, the hero remains the same (all Western heroes are ageless and uncorruptible), while his antagonist assumes many guises—that of bank robber, hired killer, gun runner, and every other incarnation of evil—in his mission of destruction. Whatever the webs of twists and variations that imaginative scriptwriters have been able to bring to the plots, the Western, in intent and structure, remains basically a morality play in which Good and Evil fight over the soul of Man.

That here could be no compromise in the hero's mission—which is to eradicate evil, as long as evil exists—is best exemplified by this exchange in *Tex Thorne*. To the girl, Susan Locke, who is entreating him to go back to his hometown and rid it of its resident outlaw, Tex answers: "I don't want to go back to Dewdrop;" at which point the hero's moral dilemma is clearly posited by Susan: "I know how you feel, Tex, but if you don't face Colt Ashton it'll dog your tracks all over the range!"

All Western villains are not as fiendish as Colt Ashton, of course, but their villainy sets them apart from the common folks, as much as the hero's valor does; not because they are better or worse than the common man, but because they are single-minded in their life pursuits. Western villains never know when to quit (and this is often their undoing), but, like the hero, they go on, bound by a compulsion they cannot fight, or even understand. It can be said that they evidence an ineluctable tropism towards evil, just as the hero manifests an irresistible attraction towards good.

While this seems self-evident it is important to note that, in the Western comics, the action is almost always initiated by the villain. King is sent out on his dangerous errands in answer to some menace, Red Ryder would hire on as stagecoach driver in order to smoke out a gang of crooked road agents, or the Cisco Kid would chance upon a holdup in progress. In other cases the villain triggers the action even more directly by trying to murder the hero as the opening gambit in some sinister scheme. The number of times that evildoers of every stripe and description have tried to do in the Lone Ranger, for instance, is simply staggering. They should have known better, of course, but the antagonist's mortal flaw is his arrogance—*hubris* in its most naked manifestation.

The most basic motivation for villainy is greed in all its forms—for gold, for land, for power. In a country as open as the Old West, the possibilities were endless. Unscrupulous ranchers would brand their neighbor's cattle as their own, shyster lawyers would defraud old widows and young orphans alike, claim jumpers would cheat a prospector out of his gold pickings. In the course of his dark undertakings, the villain would often routinely dispose of a number of opponents by the simple expedient of shooting them down. (Because of the outcries from squeamish critics the victims would, in later years, be dispatched off-stage, as in a classical play). Murder, however, was traditionally seen with a more detached eye in the West than in less rugged settings. In *Red Ryder*, an obviously jaded circuit-riding judge (not a little reminiscent of the real Judge Bean) tut-tuts Red's charges of attempted murder against a pair of outlaws ("You're alive, aint'cha?"), but rises with indignation upon learning that the duo has also tried to steal Red's horse!

While they often exhibit the same bravery, daring and skill as the hero, the villains differ in one enormously important respect: unlike the hero, who is tied to a code of chivalry, the villains are always ready to use every means at their disposal to achieve their ends. It can be said, without irony, that the difference lies in the villain's pragmatic approach, as opposed to the hero's dogmatic attitude. One of the villain's chief stratagems is to get in cahoots with some of the local authorities (sheriff, marshal, mayor, judge, or whoever), therefore forcing the hero into going outside the law. The ambiguity is not lost on the readers who can thus vicariously enjoy the dual thrill of being both hunter and hunted.

Morris, *Lucky Luke*. Real-life villains make frequent appearances in this Western parody. © Éditions Dupuis.

In the comic strip Westerns, unlike the movie Westerns, real-life villains have made only rare appearances. Billy the Kid was sighted from a distance in *Wild Bill Pecos*, and the James brothers were occasionally referred to in *The Outlaw Kid*. Joaquin Murrieta made a brief—if gruesome—appearance in *Texas Slim*; but, by and large, authentic outlaws of the Old West have been largely ignored in American Westerns. Not so in Europe, where cartoonists are more given to name-dropping, and where Morris and Goscinny, chief among them, have made excellent periodic use of such certified Western badmen as Billy

SIMULANT L'ÉVANOUISSEMENT ET SENTANT LE FER ROUGE PRES DE SON VISAGE, DANS UN SUPRÊME EFFORT, IL SE RAIDIT ET AVEC SA MAIN DROITE RESTÉE LIBRE, IL PREND UNE POIGNÉE DE SABLE

Fred Harman, *Bronc Peeler*. The hero is about to be tortured by his Mexican enemy.
© Fred Harman.

the Kid, the Dalton brothers, Jesse James and Black Bart in *Lucky Luke*.

Most of the villains in Western comics have been individuals engaged on a course of evil for personal reasons. From time to time, however, some ethnic groups have been singled out, and while not common, the practice was by no means unusual, although it has been considerably whittled down in recent times.

No group in the comics has been maligned as much as the Mexicans. The villains in several of Mickey Mouse's Western adventures sported definite Spanish surnames as well as stereotyped Latin mannerisms (such as Don Jollio, oily, flowery and bemoustached, ensconced in tight pants and wide sombrero). Raised in the southwest, Fred Harman displayed some of the prejudices of the region in his strips: some of his more despicable villains were Mexicans. In *Bronc Peeler* the hero rescued a lovely señorita from the clutches of the snarling Carlos who then lured the cowboy into a dastardly ambush, and proceeded to torture him with a red-hot branding iron. In *Red Ryder* there was the instance (among many) when Red put an end to the depredations of a murderous gang of bandidos led by a swarthy and depraved character known as Yaqui Joe.

These two episodes took place in the Thirties. In a 1939 *Lone Ranger* sequence (the last one signed by Ed Kressy, incidentally), on the other hand, the Lone Ranger joined forces with wealthy ranch owner Don

Cesar against a pillaging ring of outlaws operating on both sides of the border. "For Texas and for Mexico!," they shouted before marching into battle, in a weird show of pan-American solidarity, one full year before the official inauguration of the "good neighbor policy." In recent times the Mexican has joined his Indian counterpart as the hero's sidekick in such disparate strips as *The Cisco Kid* and *Jerry Spring*.

Indians have been treated somewhat differently in Western comics. While there has been an occasional Indian villain in comic strips, these were not singled out as such. The Indian menace was always portrayed as collective: the Apaches, Navahos, Comanches and Cheyennes seen ambushing wagon trains, attacking white settlers, and raiding isolated army outposts did so *en masse* in a vast display of primitive, demonic and blind destructiveness. Their legitimate grievances were seldom explained, or were distorted. Whereas the outlaws, desperadoes and assorted villains of the Western frontier were shown as the outriders of Evil, the Indians were for a long time depicted as the legions of doom, the modern embodiments of the horsemen of the Apocalypse.

Rino Albertarelli, *I Protagonisti*. The red menace. © Daim Press.

During World War II the role was taken over by the minions of the Axis powers. Japanese saboteurs and Nazi agents became the collective menace in *Tom Mix*, *Little Joe,* or *Gene Autry*. There was a similar trend in the movies of the time (remember *Cowboy Commandos* or *Texas to Bataan*, with the "Range Busters"?), but it lasted only as long as the war.

Towards a mythography of the West

In the opening paragraph of his splendid study of Western history and legend, *The Westerners*, Dee Brown writes:

"The story of the American West has all the elements of the *Iliad* and *Odyssey*. It is a heroic world of quests and wars, of journeyings into remote lands, of daring hunts, last stands, and legendary exploits. It is an epic of mighty deeds, of triumphs and failures, of inconsistent heroes and heroines. The West is a tragedy relieved by interludes of comedy. It is a tale of good and evil, a morality play of personified abstractions. Only an epic poet, a Homer, could encompass the American West and sing its essence in one compact volume."

The Western has failed to produce the one Homer wished for by Dee Brown, but the mythology of the West has come down to us through many voices: those of dime novelists, of historians and chroniclers, of dramatists and musical comedy writers. Above all

Charles Flanders, *The Lone Ranger*. Born on radio the Lone Ranger owes his fame, in great part, to the movie and comic strip versions. © King Features Syndicate.

else it has come down to us through the movies (and television), and through the comics, as a kind of pictorial mythography that has been unfolding before our eyes all throughout this century. It is only fitting that the most universally accepted myth of modern times should have been upheld, most of all, by the two genuine art forms of the century.

Western movies and Western comics are directly inter-related in many significant ways. Instant recognition of this symbiotic relationship comes from examining the adaptation from one medium to the other. Western heroes have always crossed with ease from celluloid to newsprint, and vice-versa. *King of the Royal Mounted* was made into a movie serial in 1942, for instance, and *Red Ryder* was transposed to the screen no less than 22 times. Some of the actors who played the role of the red-haired cowboy have included Don Barry, Wild Bill Elliott, Allan Lane and Jim Bannon. That the stupefying range of physiognomies and acting styles represented by this array did not detract from Red Ryder's public acceptance is a tribute to the solidity of the hero created by Fred Harman.

The Lone Ranger was born over the radio waves, but his strongest impersonation came from the original movie version and from the *Lone Ranger* newspaper strip, both originated in the same year (1938). Likewise the fame of the Cisco Kid was mainly fanned

Al McKimson, *Roy Rogers*. Like other Western movie stars before him, Roy Rogers made an easy transition from screen to newsprint. © King Features Syndicate.

Chris Kenyon, *Bonanza!* The Cartwright family transposed from the TV screen to the newspaper strip. © Chronicle Features Syndicate.

by the numerous film adaptations of the character, and by Salinas's stunning comic strip artwork.

In Spain, *El Coyote* (first portrayed in novels) was further popularized by its famous comic strip adaptation, and by the subsequent motion pictures that derived from it. The same happened with *Alma Grande* and *El Payo* in Mexico.

The transposition from film to comic strip or comic book has been even more common. Certainly Tom Mix's fame would not have survived to this day, if it had only been for his movies (most of which were silent, and all of which are rarely seen on television). The many comic strips based on his fictional career, here and abroad, have contributed to keep his legend alive. The same holds true for other Western stars, from Gene Autry to Roy Rogers and Allan "Rocky" Lane, whose reputations have become firmly entrenched in the public mind, partly because of their comic book impersonations. The strongest case is that of Hopalong Cassidy: it can be argued that Dan Spiegle's version equals, and sometimes surpasses, the *Hopalong Cassidy* film series, many of which were routine shoot'em-ups, without Spiegle's depth of perception.

The latest film medium—television—has also mightily contributed to comic art Westerns as a source of inspiration. *Maverick* in the United States, and *Gun Law* (based on *Gunsmoke*) in England are the best known and most worthwhile examples; but most Western TV series have found their comic counterparts: *Bonanza*, *Wagon Train*, *Have Gun Will Travel*, *The Rifleman* have all been transposed to comic books, with mixed results.

Fred Sande (S.M. "Jerry" Iger) and Jack Kirby, *Wilton of the West*. There always was a strong relationship between Western comics and movies. © S.M. Iger.

Beyond the formal borrowings that have always taken place between films and comics lies, however, a much deeper and more meaningful relationship. The Western movie classics of the Thirties, Forties and Fifties have had a tremendous impact on Western cartoonists, and shots from such acknowledged masterpieces of the genre as *Stagecoach*, *Red River*, *Bend of the River* and *Man Without a Star* have cropped up in many a Western strip, here and abroad. Conversely the traditional image of the Western hero has found its most consistent incarnation in the comics, and this has served the Western movie makers as a kind of ideographic shorthand.

Between Western films and Western comics there exists a shred continuum of traditions and conventions, a common vocabulary of images, and a congruent syntax of sequences. The forms of Western movies and Western comics can easily be transposed from one medium to the other, and intuitively understood by both. Together they have become the most important contribution to the Western mythos. No understanding of the West, its implications, resonances and extensions as a living mythology, can be arrived at without knowledge and study of Western films and of Western comics.

Jijé, *Le Spécialiste*. This short-lived Western strip was strongly influenced by movie techniques. © Jijé.

© Dargaud

BIBLIOGRAPHY

The literature on the specific subject of Western comics is practically nonexistent. The purpose of this bibliography is therefore twofold: a) to indicate the sources mentioned in this book, and b) to provide a basic list of background material on the comics and the American West.

I—WORKS MENTIONED IN THE TEXT

Ainsworth, Ed, *The Cowboy in Art*, New York: World Publishing, 1968.

Brown, Dee, *The Westerners*, New York: Holt, Rinehart and Winston, 1974.

Fenin, George, and Everson, William, *The Western* (revised edition), New York: Grossman Publishers, 1973.

Greg, Michel, "Le roi de la police montée," in: *Giff-Wiff*, No. 9, Paris, March 1964.

Harman, Fred, "New Tracks in Old Trails," in: *True West*, No. 89, Austin, Tex., September-October 1968.

Harmon, Jim, *Nostalgia Catalogue*, Los Angeles: J.P. Tarcher, 1973.

Horn, Maurice, ed., *The World Encyclopedia of Comics*, New York: Chelsea House, 1976.

Watrous, George R., *The History of Winchester Firearms* (fourth edition), New York: Winchester Press, 1975.

West, Gordon, "J.R. Williams, Cowboy Cartoonist," in: *Frontier Times*, Austin, Tex., December-January 1971.

Williams, James Robert, *Cowboys Out Our Way*, New York: Scribners, 1946.

II—OTHER REFERENCE SOURCES
a) *on the comics*

Becker, Stephen, *Comic Art in America*, New York: Simon and Schuster, 1959.

Couperie, Pierre, and Horn, Maurice, *A History of the Comic Strip*, New York: Crown Publishers, 1968.

Gasca, Luis, *Los Comics en España*, Barcelona: Editorial Lumen, 1969.

Goulart, Ron, *The Adventurous Decade*, New Rochelle, N.Y.: Arlington House, 1975.

Overstreet, Bob, *The Comic Book Price Guide* (sixth edition), Cleveland, Tenn.: Bob Overstreet, 1976.

Reitberger, Reinhold, and Fuchs, Wolfgang, *Comics: Anatomy of a Mass Medium*, Boston: Little, Brown, 1972.

Rustemagić, Ervin, "La Bande Dessinée Yougoslave," in: *Phénix*, No. 38, Paris, June 1974.

Strazzula, Gaetano, *I Fumetti*, Florence: Sansoni, 1970.

Tercinet, Alain, "Red Ryder, ou l'Ouest bien défini," in: *Giff-Wiff*, No. 11, Paris, September 1964.

Waugh, Coulton, *The Comics*, New York: Macmillan, 1947.

b) on the American West

Billington, Ray, *Westward Expansion*, New York: Macmillan, 1967.

Blacker, Irwin R., ed., *The Old West in Fact*, New York: Ivan Obolensky, 1961.

Brown, Dee, *Bury My Heart at Wounded Knee*, New York: Holt, Rinehart and Winston, 1971.

Clark, Thomas D., *Frontier America*, New York: Scribners, 1969.

Cody, Louisa, *Memoirs of Buffalo Bill*, New York: D. Appleton & Company, 1919.

Ewers, John C., *Artists of the Old West*, Garden City, N.Y.: Doubleday, 1965.

Hassrick, Royal B., *Cowboys*, London: Octopus Books, 1974.

Lavender, David, *The American Heritage Book of the Great West*, New York: American Heritage Publishers, 1965.

Nye, W.S., *Carbine and Lance*, Norman, Okla.: University of Oklahoma Press, 1937.

Riegel, Robert E., and Athearn, Robert G., *America Moves West*, New York: Holt, Rinehart and Winston, 1956.

INDEX

Boldface numbers refer to illustrations.
The color section follows page 128.